The Intonation Systems of English

Andrew Linn
Luton 1996

The Intonation Systems of English

PAUL TENCH

CASSELL

Cassell
Wellington House, 125 Strand, London WC2R 0BB
127 West 24th Street, New York, NY 10011

First published 1996

British Library Cataloguing in Publication Data
A catalogue record for this book is available from the British Library.

ISBN 0-304-33690-4 (hardback)
        0-304-33691-2 (paperback)

Library of Congress Cataloging-in-Publication Data
Tench, Paul.
   The intonation systems of English / Paul Tench.
     p. cm.
   Includes bibliographical references and index.
   ISBN 0-304-33690-4. — ISBN 0-304-33691-2 (pbk.)
   1. English language—Intonation. I. Title.
PE1139.5.T46 1996
421'.6—dc20   95-52675
                    CIP

Typeset by Ben Cracknell Studios
Printed and bound in Great Britain by Biddles Ltd, Guildford and King's Lynn

Contents

Preface

1995 marked – It seems incredible – the fiftieth anniversary of Kenneth Pike's publication of *The Intonation of American English*. It is a classic; it is systematic and comprehensive to an extent not remotely matched by any subsequent scholar of American intonation.

1995 marked – and this seems almost as incredible – the twenty-fifth anniversary of M. A. K. Halliday's *A Course in Spoken English: Intonation*. This too provides a thorough coverage, but of British RP intonation.

In their different ways, Pike and Halliday have been the inspiration behind this book. Pike's work, in my estimation, is seriously under-rated as a comprehensive descriptive statement of an essential feature of language. To Halliday, I owe the debt of an insight into the place that intonation holds in an integrative view of language. My own aim has been to produce a comprehensive descriptive statement of British RP intonation within an integrative view of spoken discourse.

I owe debts elsewhere: to David Crystal's *Prosodic Systems and Intonation in English*, which is still the most useful account of the phonetics of English intonation, and to other writers on intonation like Brazil, Brown, Cruttenden and Ladd. I owe a debt to Robin Fawcett and Barrie Wynn for their encouragements in my work. And last, but certainly not least, I owe debts to Julia Bullough, Ann Parry, Cristina Rita and Jean Verrier for their patient work on the manuscript.

Acknowledgements

The author and publishers are grateful for permission to reproduce the following:

Extracts from D. Crystal and D. Davy, *Advanced Conversational English* (Longman, 1975): by permission of Professor David Crystal.

Figure on p. 49, from G. Brown, K.L. Currie and J. Kenworthy, *Questions of Intonation* (Croom Helm, 1980): by permission of Routledge.

Figure 3.1, from David L.E. Watt, 'An instrumental analysis of English nuclear tones' in P. Tench (ed.), *Studies in Systemic Phonology* (Pinter, 1992): by permission of Dr David Watt.

Figure 4.1, from Louis Alexander, *First Things First* (Longman, 1967): by permission of Longman Group Limited.

Figure 5.2, from M. Liberman, *The Intonational System of English* (Garland, 1979).

1

Intonation

WHAT IT IS AND WHAT IT DOES

Intonation refers to the rise and fall of the pitch of the voice in spoken language. When you say something, you cannot say it without some kind of intonation – even a monotone can be classed as a kind of intonation. Intonation is inevitable in speech.

It is also important: we have all made an observation like 'It is not what they said, but the way they said it'. The 'way they said it' is a rough guide to what intonation is.

Language students and teachers will also find intonation of interest as it is part of the structure of any particular language. People can hear that the intonation of English is different from the intonation of French, or German, or Russian or any other European language, and is decidedly very different from the intonation of Japanese, Hindi, Swahili, Quechua and all the other non-European languages of the world. Furthermore, the intonation of English varies within the range of national and regional accents that we recognize: the so-called drawl of Southern USA intonation is quite distinct from the melody of Welsh English intonation; and the intonation of Scottish, Irish and Liverpudlian English seems to have rises where others have falls, and vice versa. People are thus aware of intonation in a very general way, even though the details of it are not properly appreciated.

Intonation has traditionally not had the same kind of attention in the past that has been accorded to the study of consonants, vowels and word stress. Rhythm has also been the focus of attention to a greater extent than intonation because of its crucial role in poetry. But in the last two decades, linguists have been turning to intonation in a much more systematic fashion as a result of the upsurge of interest in discourse studies, and as a result, much more is now known.

People have always been very much aware of consonants and vowels because, in the written form, they are the units of pronunciation that are most readily identified – even though there is an enormous discrepancy between spelling and pronunciation (as is the case, for instance, in English, French and Irish). And because we write in units of words, people also seem to be aware of word stress: people know the normal stress pattern of words: *return* has the second syllable stressed, but *hospital* the first and *cigarette* the last. Many people are aware of alternative stress patterns in modern English in words like *controversy, contribute* and *harass*. But people are much less able to talk confidently about intonation and rhythm because these are features of language in use rather than of language in units (like words). Although people can recognize the significance of the 'way' something was said, there isn't the same certainty in talking about intonation as there is about talking about words and their pronunciation.

This book is intended to introduce to language students and teachers a description of English intonation that will take into account the actual nature of intonation and its functions in spoken language. Intonation is in fact part and parcel of the English language, as it is for every language of the world. Intonation is **inevitable** whenever a language is spoken; it is **important**, because we eventually realize that it carries meaning and will often be the most important part of a message (consider *Oh they did, did they* spoken in a menacing way); and it is **integral** to the study of any language, for it links up not only with meaning, but also with grammar, pronunciation and spoken discourse at large.

1. Definition

A firmer definition than the one we gave on the first line of this chapter is that intonation is the linguistic use of pitch in utterances. By saying linguistic, we hope to avoid reference to other uses of pitch such as singing, and to subjective, aesthetic evaluations about how 'nice' and 'pleasant' (or 'ugly' and 'unpleasant') an accent's intonation is. (Some people say that they cannot stand a certain accent and its intonation; this is obviously not a linguistic judgement, since the allegedly 'unpleasant' accent still has all the forms and functions of intonation that it needs in order to carry meaning.)

We also specify **pitch** as the essence of intonation, and in this way we make intonation distinct from the broader concept of paralanguage. Intonation does in fact have both a linguistic and a paralinguistic dimension. The **linguistic dimension** concerns the message itself: how many pieces of information there are; what information is new; whether the message is complete or incomplete; whether the speaker is telling you something or asking you, or whether the speaker is turning to a new topic or finishing off an old one. The **paralinguistic dimension** concerns the messenger rather than the message: the speaker's state of mind, their degree of politeness and their effort to associate or dissociate from you. But paralanguage – and this is the point – involves not only pitch, but also volume, tempo and voice quality, indeed all the vocal effects that are available within a given language community, effects like giggling, sobbing, tut-tutting, husky voice, speaking 'through the teeth' and many, many more. Intonation itself is confined to the use of pitch alone. Whereas we will attempt to cover both the linguistic and the paralinguistic dimensions of intonation in this book, we will not be attempting to cover the whole of paralanguage.

Our definition further specifies that Intonation is concerned with utterances. This is important to note, because pitch variation is used to help signify words in many languages. If a language uses pitch variation to differentiate between words, we call that language a **tone language**. There are many examples of tone languages in the world; indeed maybe up to 50 per cent of the world's languages are tone languages. Chinese is a well-known example: if you take a word like *ma*, it could mean different things depending on whether it was spoken on a low pitch, a high pitch, a mid pitch, a falling pitch or a rising pitch. Here is an example from another tone language, Thai: these are five different words which could all be spelt *kha*, as far as consonants and vowels are concerned. However, if *kha* is pronounced with a low pitch, it means *spice*; if it is pronounced with a high pitch, it means *trade*; with a mid pitch, *herb*; with a falling pitch, *kill*; and with a rising pitch, *leg*:

(1.1)   _ kha = spice
           ⁻ kha = trade
           – kha = herb
           \ kha = kill
           / kha = leg

It may be tempting to seek some kind of semantic link between the meanings (e.g. *spice* and *herb*), but that would be quite fortuitous, as *trade*, *kill* and *leg* testify.

These five different pitch variations are in contrast with each other and help to differentiate word meanings; linguistically, these contrasting pitch variations are called **tones**, and because their function is to identify words, they can be more specifically called **lexical tones**. Their contrastive function can be compared to the contrastive function of phonemes, cf. the contrast between /l/ and /r/ in English, in *lamb* and *ram*. In fact, their contrastive function is more akin to the contrastive function of word stress in a language like English, of *insight* /'ɪnsaɪt/ and *incite* /ɪn'saɪt/, and words like *invalid*, *entrance* and all the noun/verb pairs like *import*, *survey*, *accent*, etc. A well-known word-stress contrast is found in Spanish: *término* (= 'end' (noun)), *termino* (= 'I finish') and *terminó* (= 'he/she/it finished'). A tone language does not usually have word-stress contrasts as well, and languages that employ word-stress as a means of lexical contrast do not usually have a comprehensive system of lexical tone contrasts.

Our definition of intonation has thus to make clear the difference between pitch being used for lexical tone, and pitch being used for intonation purposes. We shall now illustrate the latter. If you say

(1.2)   John's going out, isn't he

with a falling pitch on *isn't he*, it will sound as if you are pretty sure of your facts. However, if you say the very same utterance with a rising pitch on *isn't he*, you will sound as if you are not so sure of your facts. Say (1.2) in these two ways and check your impressions: going down on *isn't he* should give you an impression of certainty, going up an impression of uncertainty, even of questioning.

Notice that the words are the same in both cases and that the difference in meaning is solely a matter of pitch variation. This is parallel to the Thai example in (1.1) where the consonants and the vowel are constant and the difference in meaning is solely a matter of the pitch variation. The distinction between the Thai example and the English example is obvious: whereas the Thai example concerns differences in words (i.e. lexical tone), the English example concerns differences in utterances (i.e. intonation). Intonation is thus the linguistic use of pitch in utterances.

Three more points need to be made, to prevent possible confusion. The first is this: very often, utterances consist of single words like *Yes, No, Well, Right, Excellent, Bother!* and so on. These single-word utterances will take a range of intonations: *Yes* with a falling pitch will sound like a definite statement of agreement in response to a question; *Yes* with a rising pitch will sound like agreement with what somebody else is saying, without interrupting them; and *Yes* with a fall and then a rise all within the single word will sound as if you only half-agree. Say these three variations to yourself; no doubt you will be able to think of many more variations. Try to work out their differences in meaning. However, note this: the basic meaning of *Yes* has not changed; it retains its basic meaning of agreement throughout. It is not like the case of Thai *kha* which has radical differences of meaning. English *Yes* retains its basic meaning; what changes is its effect on the dialogue. If someone asks you a question and you reply *Yes* with a falling pitch, that signals to the other person that you are in agreement with them, and because there is assured common ground between you, the other person can go on to a new point. If, however, you reply by saying *Yes* with a falling-rising pitch, that signals that while you do agree to a certain extent, you do not do so whole-heartedly; this will probably have the effect on the other person of feeling the need to backtrack, or modify their argument, or think of new ways of trying to convince you. Your intonation of *Yes* will have an effect on the way the conversation proceeds.

The point being made here is that although the differences of pitch can fall on a single word in English, it is a distinctly different matter from the lexical tone of a language like Thai. It just so happens that in these cases the utterance consists of a single word, but because that one word has constituted a whole utterance, it is subject to the inevitability, i.e. the ever-present nature, of intonation.

If, instead of replying *Yes*, you had replied *I agree*, the same intonation patterns could have applied. You could have said *I agree* with the same kind of falling pitch to indicate a definite statement, or with the same kind of falling-rising pitch on -*gree* to indicate half-agreement, or with the same kind of rising pitch which indicates that you do not wish to interrupt. This utterance consists of two words, and we are less tempted to think that the variation of pitch affects the meanings of the words: it clearly affects the meaning of the utterance.

You could experiment with these three patterns on other single-word utterances and check that the basic meaning of the word does not change and that the kind of meaning associated with falls and fall-rises in roughly parallel in each case; the case of rises is a little more complicated, because rises can sometimes mean 'I am going to continue' or 'I am letting you continue' on the one hand, or 'I am asking you' or 'appealing to you' on the other. But the fact that you can separate off the meaning of the intonation from the basic meaning of the word is proof that we are handling intonation in these cases and not lexical tone. (If you think about it, you cannot separate off the meaning of the pitch variation in Thai words, because it is part of the word itself – just like word-stress in English.)

The second point is that intonation is tied to utterances rather than to sentences. Spoken language is not as neat and tidy as written language. If by 'sentence', you are looking for neat, well formed structures of recognized syntactic patterns, you will not always find them in spoken language. Here is an example as recorded in Brown, Currie and Kenworthy (1980):

(1.3)   I regret + putting the people out of the out of the South Side and central Edinburgh you know ++ I don't think ++ especially after the war you know after the ++ war when they started the ++ redevelopment and the ++ well the authority more or less made it that everybody was to go outside you know ++ the gardens and houses but ++...

Why is it so confusingly unstructured? This is, nevertheless, typical of informal spontaneous conversation; it would not be typical of reading a passage aloud where all the decisions of what to say have already been taken. Brown, Currie and Kenworthy (1980: 47) explain:

> In producing spontaneous speech the speaker has to decide on a topic, select the 'staging' procedures for presenting his (*sic*) topic..., determine what he (*sic*) must introduce as new and what he can take as given, sort out the appropriate syntactic structures, select lexical items, check that his listener is following what he is saying and agreeing with it, make clear that he wishes to continue with or to give away his turn, quite apart from speaking. In spontaneous speech,

especially of a quite unrehearsed kind, where a speaker is more or less painfully working out what he wants to say as he goes along, many speakers will produce non-fluent speech.

So, it is no good expecting well-formed, precisely executed sentences in all forms of spoken language. Sometimes, the 'sentences' are so long and complicated with abandoned or half-abandoned elements, and cluttered with asides and appeals, that many, many units of intonation are employed to manage them. On the other hand, two consecutive sentences may be so short as to be contained within a single unit of intonation; it should not be too difficult to think of a situation in which the following is said quickly in one 'go':

(1.4)   He did. I saw it.

A number of intonation studies do misleadingly refer to 'sentence intonation' or 'sentence prosody'. Such studies usually confine themselves to the melodies of single sentences spoken in isolation or in a simple two-part dialogue. This is only a fraction of the reality, since spoken language is overwhelmingly longer than single sentences or two lines of dialogue; spoken language involves discourse.

The third, and final, point to be made in preventing confusion is a relatively minor one. Occasionally, a dichotomy is established between tone languages and intonation languages.[1] This is a complete misunderstanding about the nature of intonation. Some languages use pitch variation for identifying words, i.e. lexical tone; other languages, like English, don't. However, all languages use pitch variations for intonation purposes, even including all the tone languages; intonation relates to utterances and discourse, and of course, speakers of all languages (tone and non-tone languages) use their languages for utterances and discourse. You might wonder how a tone language manages to use pitch variation for lexical tone **and** intonation: what happens is that the intonation patterns are superimposed upon lexical tone, so that if the intonation pattern falls, the lexical tones – whatever they are: high, mid, low, etc. – all fall relatively lower, and so on. What is noticeable is that a tone language often has a simpler intonation system than a non-tone language, and that it will employ alternative linguistic devices – in grammar, usually – to compensate. This seems a reasonable enough assumption, so that any language's use of pitch is not overloaded.

——

2. System

Intonation is integral to languages, and therefore to language study and to language learning and teaching. Neglect of intonation in the past is now no excuse for neglect in the present. Traditionally, pronunciation manuals concentrated on consonants, vowels and word stress, and lexical tone in tone languages: this area of interest is often labelled **word phonology**. Word phonology is readily accessible to anyone with an interest in language, because words and their pronunciation are easily identifiable; their representation, through spelling, is also easily recognized in the written form of languages. (It does not matter if the language uses an alphabetic script, a syllabary, or pictographs; it is nevertheless words – as basic terms of any message – that get represented.)

Rhythm and intonation are less easy to talk about because they accompany whole messages. Rhythm is readily identifiable in poetry, but the role of intonation in the recitation of poetry is less widely acknowledged. This does not mean that no one had ever investigated the role of intonation until recently, but simply that it did not receive equivalent coverage and attention. Indeed, some eminent names in acting have drawn attention to intonation and rhythm, namely David Garrick and Joshua Steele in the eighteenth century; and some eminent linguists in the first half of this century have published interesting studies, for instance, Armstrong and Ward, Jones, H.E. Palmer and Pike. However, it was not until the availability of tape recordings that linguists were able to investigate intonation more thoroughly. The acquisition of tape recorders produced a new dimension to intonational research in the 1950s and 1960s. Although Jassem, Kingdon and O'Connor and Arnold bridge the gap between the older studies and the newer, it was Halliday and Crystal who set the pace by analysing long stretches of tape recorded spoken discourse. Not only were long stretches of spoken discourse available for listening and re-listening, but recordings could be subjected to a wide range of acoustic experimentation. The amount of information that is now available is exhaustive; theories and descriptions of intonation can now be based and verified on much more objective grounds.

Crystal (1969) is still, possibly, the most comprehensive discussion on the phonetic nature of British English intonation, but Halliday (1967) sought to present a more linguistic orientation and emphasized the phonological nature of intonation. A most important part of this emphasis was to draw attention to intonation's role in the speaker's organization of information. In previous studies, the emphasis had been primarily on the attitudinal role of intonation, i.e. how a person's feelings were expressed. Halliday, rather, drew attention to the informational role of intonation, i.e. how a person's meanings were expressed. Earlier studies had largely overlooked this aspect, H.E. Palmer being the notable exception.

The intonation systems of English

Halliday introduced the notion of a trio of systems operating in English intonation: **tonality** is the system by which a stretch of spoken text is segmented into a series of discrete units of intonation which correspond to the speaker's perception of pieces (or 'chunks') of information; **tonicity** is the system by which an individual, discrete, unit of intonation is shown to have a prominent word which indicates the focus of information; and **tone** is the system of contrasting pitch movements in each unit of intonation, which, among other roles, identifies the status of the information, e.g. major, minor or incomplete.

We should look at this concept of system more closely. In linguistic terms, a system means that there is a choice between one possibility and another, resulting in a difference of meaning. When we looked at (1.2) above, we noted that the wording could be identical for different renderings, one with a falling pitch and the other with a rising pitch. The choice of pitch represents a system. In the case of our discussion of *Yes* and *I agree*, we noted that there were at least three possible renderings, with a different meaning 'attached' to each possibility. If there is a choice of three alternatives with a meaning 'attached' to each of them, we could call that choice a three-way system – in this case, a three-way system of pitch variations (or 'tones').

Just as there is a system for tones, there are also systems for tonicity and tonality. How are you most likely to say this question?

(1.5)   What are you going to do tonight?

At a good guess, the word *do* would be the most prominent word: it is pitched quite high, but the voice drops to a low pitch which is subsequently heard in the following word. *Do* is thus the focus of information, and in any case, is likely to be the main point of interest in the question.

But say (1.5) again, with the emphasis on *tonight*. What change of meaning takes place? The words remain the same, but the main point of interest is no longer on what the person is going to do. It is as if the speaker is indicating that he or she knows what the person might be doing in the afternoon or tomorrow evening, etc., or what the person had done the night before, etc., but in contrast to these points of time, the interest of the question now lies in what the person plans to do *tonight*.

Now, you could make the word *you* the focal point, and again you could consider what change of meaning takes place. It is as if the speaker is alluding to the fact that they know what they are going to do, but now wants to know what you, i.e. the addressee, in contrast to everybody else, plan to do.

Can you think of changes of meaning that are caused by making *going* or *are* prominent (or even, possibly, *what*)? This illustrates the tonicity system: if you change the prominent word, you change the focus of information, and thus create a different meaning. The tonicity system relates to the choice of prominent word.

Tonality is also subject to a system. If you change the number of intonation units, you change the number of pieces of information. You could say (1.6) as one piece of information:

(1.6)   I'm going into town this morning

but you could present it as two pieces of information by separating off *this morning* with a little pause and saying:

(1.7)   I'm going into town | this morning

This sounds as if you have given one piece of information, and then, possibly even as an afterthought, added an extra piece of information to indicate when you were off to town. This would entail making *town* prominent, and then, secondly, *morning* prominent as well. The difference between (1.6) and (1.7) is simply the speaker's perception of the message as either one piece of information or two. (You might argue that (1.7) would have a comma after *town*; but remember we are talking about **spoken** discourse; commas belong to **written** discourse.)

The tonality system also links up with certain syntactic choices in English. There is a difference in meaning and in grammar between (1.8) and (1.9).

(1.8)   My brother who lives in Nairobi...

(1.9)   My brother | who lives in Nairobi...

In (1.8) there is no pause before *who*, and the relative clause tells you which brother the speaker is talking about, i.e. not the brother who lives anywhere else; the relative clause defines which brother; it restricts the referent. In (1.9), with a pause before *who*, the relative clause does not define or restrict; it adds an extra piece of information. The difference in tonality – whether there is a single unit of intonation in (1.8) or two in (1.9) – matches a difference in grammar, and also a difference in meaning; (1.8) implies that there are other brothers, (1.9) does not.

This book will devote a considerable amount of space to describing these three systems of English intonation. The description of the intonation in terms of systems shows that intonation is as systematic as other parts of the phonology. And because it is systematic, it can be presented in terms of differences of meaning, and that in turn implies that intonation can be taught and learned. There is no need to think of intonation as a nebulous phenomenon that can only be appreciated in subjective, emotional terms, and is so personal that it defies careful analysis. On the contrary, although there is a personal, subjective, emotional element to it, intonation is mainly conventional. If it was not conventional, we could never know what meanings it conveys; in order to interpret an intonation's meaning, we have to assume that the intonation pattern that one person uses means the same thing when somebody else uses it. To take a simple example, how do we know that an intonation pattern is a menacing one if we don't have an 'agreement' (or convention) that that is what that particular pattern means? It is because intonation is conventional and we know what different patterns mean that we can make the comment about not liking the 'way' something was said. And because there is conventionality about intonation, we can analyse it reasonably objectively and describe it reasonably succinctly

Before we leave this concept of system there is one other major point to be made. We shall be concentrating on a description of English intonation in this book and on the tonality, tonicity and tone systems in particular. But just as each language has its own system of consonants and vowels and word stress (and lexical tones), each language has its own system of intonation. This is partly why the intonations of different languages sound different; although there are other features that affect the overall sound of the language, like voice quality, the patterns of intonation are distinctively different too.

Each language has its own system of intonation. It seems inevitable that each language will manifest tonality, tonicity and tones, but the way they do so will vary considerably. (We say 'will manifest' and 'will vary', because only relatively few languages have ever had their intonation system investigated in any detail, and those that have, suggest that the kind of variety displayed will be applicable to all languages.) It seems inevitable, also, that each language will manifest a system of tone contrasts, but not necessarily a system in tonicity and tonality. In Hausa, a language of West Africa, for example, the prominent word in an intonation unit is always the last one; in other words, there is no possibility of variation as in English, and thus no possibility of choice: no choice, no system. It is conceivable, too, that a language might have a fixed structure in tonality, too, in which case again the same principle applies: no choice, no system. What this means, simply, is that the kinds of meaning that are conveyed in English by choices in tonicity and tonality are conveyed in other languages by other means – usually grammatical, but by lexical means as well.

The next point to make in this comparison of the intonation systems in different languages is that similar sounding patterns in two languages might possibly convey different meanings, just as similar meanings might be conveyed by different patterns. I remember overhearing a conversation between a German lady and a British lady who had moved to Germany. It sounded as if they were going for each other hammer and tongs, and I even wondered whether I should intervene. However, I had no need to worry because the door opened and the British lady beamed: 'Schwester A. is such a darling!' The mistake I had made was to interpret German intonation in terms of my English intonation, and I had come to the wrong conclusion.

In the same way that we can misinterpret the intonation of another language, we can also mis-produce it when we are speaking in another language. When you are still in the early stages of learning to speak in a new language, it is often difficult to reproduce the new intonation and 'sound' right. I remember learning Welsh but having difficulty in adjusting from an English intonation to a Welsh one. This is a difficulty that most learners of a foreign language have; if they are conscious of it, there is a good chance of correct adjustments; if they are not aware of it, then of course intonation will remain a problem.

But is faulty intonation a problem? It often is, but not always. What is very noticeable is the tolerance that native speakers show when a learner fumbles over consonants, vowels and word stress (and even lexical tone in tone languages). This tolerance derives from the native speaker's awareness of word phonology and possibly from their familiarity with other learners' efforts (or indeed their own) of the problems of pronouncing the words of another language. But such tolerance does not always extend to intonation, for two reasons. Firstly, native speakers are not usually so aware of intonation, a point that we have made before. But secondly, and possibly more alarmingly, a mistaken intonation still **means** something; it might well be that you intended to convey one particular meaning but they interpreted it quite differently. This is how misunderstandings of national character can get perpetuated; for instance, the normal information-giving intonation of one language might happen to coincide with the intonation of arrogance in another. This could, quite clearly, lead people into thinking that the others actually **are** arrogant, because they 'sound' arrogant. Misunderstandings can happen in other areas too: people who are giving information might sound as if they are always checking up to see if you have understood them, and so sound patronizing. Others who do not adjust the words of prominence in their own intonation units will have difficulty in doing so when they speak English, with the effect that a British person might misinterpret the real focus of information and the ensuing discourse get miscued.

The problem is that mistaken intonation patterns still mean something, but obviously not the intended meaning, and so misunderstandings can easily follow. It seems important, therefore, for learners to adjust to the system of their target languages, and for native speakers to become aware of the system that they themselves use, albeit unconsciously, in their own language.

———

3. Structure

The intonation of English not only displays system, it also displays structure. Indeed, structures of some kind will be found in all intonation systems in the world's languages. Think again of the question in

(1.5)   What are you going to do tonight?

or the statement in

(1.6)   I'm going into town this morning

each being said in one 'go'. Each is considered as a unit of intonation, each handling one piece of information (whether asking about it or stating it). Then, think again of the statement in

(1.7)   I'm going into town | this morning

being said in two 'goes'. In this case, **each** part is a unit of intonation: one piece of information is given in the first unit, a second piece in the second. In the same way, the part of the utterance given in (1.8) is a single unit of intonation, whereas the same wording in (1.9) is a sequence of two units: the first unit of (1.9) simply gives the topic (*My brother*) and the second provides an extra piece of information about the topic.

Each intonation unit has a structure; we will illustrate the intonation unit structure first of all with a very familiar saying:

(1.10)   A dog is a man's best friend

Imagine, perhaps, that someone says this just as the conversation turns to the topic of dogs. It is most likely to be said as a single unit of intonation, with the word *friend* being most prominent, and the pitch of the voice falling to a low level on that word. (Notice we have then specified all three systems: tonality (segmentation of the discourse into units of intonation) = one unit; tonicity (identification of the most prominent word within the unit) = *friend*; tone (specification of the contrastive pitch movement) = falling.) In (1.10), the word *friend* is said to be the 'nucleus' or the 'tonic syllable'. These two terms represent two traditions in the description of intonation; in this context they mean the same thing, as shown in Table 1.1. The part of the utterance up to *best* is called the 'pre-tonic segment', which in turn can be divided into the 'pre-head' and the 'head'. The head is the part which begins with the first stressed syllable, known as the 'onset' syllable, in this case the word *dog*; the word *a* before *dog* is unstressed and precedes the head, hence its label 'pre-head'. The structure is thus:

pre-tonic segment		tonic/nucleus
pre-head	head	
A	'dog is a 'man's 'best	'friend

TABLE 1.1

The stressed syllables are traditionally marked by '; the tonic or nucleus is marked either in bold, or in capitals or, as we shall do, by underlining.

The tonic (or nucleus) is obligatory, because it is that part of the intonation unit that bears the contrastive pitch movement, the tone; it is also always stressed not only because it bears the tone but also because of its essential prominence. The other parts of the unit are optional, in the sense that they may or may not happen to be present.

The sentiment of (1.10) could easily be rendered as

(1.11)   'Dogs are 'men's 'best '<u>friends</u>

in which case there is no pre-head, because there happens to be no unstressed syllable before the onset syllable of the head (*Dogs*).

Now suppose the topic of the conversation had been different, say, horses, and somebody claimed that in fact horses were men's best friends. Another could retort:

(1.12)   '<u>Dogs</u> are 'men's 'best 'friends

with contrastive emphasis on *Dogs* right at the beginning of the intonation unit. In (1.12), *Dogs* is the most prominent; it is, therefore, the tonic (nucleus) and is not preceded by anything; therefore, in the case of (1.12), there is no pre-tonic segment, no head, and no pre-head.

What about the words that follow *Dogs* in (1.12)? The tonic (nucleus) and all following words in the same unit are collectively known as the 'tonic segment' (obviously, in contrast to the pre-tonic segment). The tonic segment can then be subdivided into the tonic and the tail. The tail thus refers to all the words subsequent to the tonic syllable. (The use of the term 'tail' and the choice of topics in (1.10), (1.11) and (1.12) are purely co-incidental!)

You might ask why it is necessary to identify so many points in the structure of the intonation unit. The answer is that different pitch movements can contrast with each other at each point of structure, and thus produce changes of meaning. The pitch of the pre-head may be either higher or lower than normal, and these variations have a significance; the pitch movement in the head is capable of many variations and these, too, have their significance; the pitch movement at the tonic provides the basis of the tone system, and the tone has an effect on the pitch of the tail. The sole purpose of this elaborate dissection of the intonation unit is to indicate the points or areas where intonation can vary and produce differences of meaning. It is the explication of the choices in meaning that determines the essence of linguistic structures.

In response to (1.12) – the contrastive assertion that it is dogs who are men's best friends – someone might agree by saying

(1.13)   yes | they are | aren't they

There are three units here (three 'goes').

(1.13a)   <u>yes</u>

stands all by itself; it consists of a tonic, but no head, pre-head, or tail.

(1.13b)   they <u>are</u>

consists of a tonic and a pre-head. It may be thought strange to have a structure that contains a pre-head, but no head, but it is perfectly possible. In (1.13b), there is no onset syllable preceding the tone; *they* is unstressed and therefore does not constitute an onset syllable. Without an onset syllable, there is no head. What this means is that the variations of meaning associated with the head are simply not available to (1.13b). (They were not available to (1.13a) either.) (1.13b) also lacks a tail.

(1.13c)   <u>aren't</u> they

has the obligatory tonic, has also a tail, but no head, and no pre-head. It will be seen how the tonic is obligatory and the head, pre-head and tail are optional. If the latter happen to be present in an intonation unit, they constitute points or areas where choices of intonation (and, therefore, choices of meaning) are potential. The choice of tone (and meaning) at the tonic is **always** realized.

The formal structure of the intonation unit is displayed in Table 1.2.

	pre-tonic segment		tonic segment	
	pre-head	head	tonic/nucleus	tail
1.10	A	'dog is a 'man's 'best	<u>friend</u>	
1.11		'Dogs are 'men's 'best	<u>friends</u>	
1.12			<u>Dogs</u>	are 'men's 'best 'friends
1.13a			<u>yes</u>	
1.13b	they		<u>are</u>	
1.13c			<u>aren't</u>	they

TABLE 1.2

One final, small theoretical point. The structure of the intonation unit has been presented mainly in terms of words so far; the tonic is the most prominent word, the tail consists of the words following the tonic, and the pre-tonic segment refers to the words preceding the tonic. We have also had recourse to refer to syllables, stressed and unstressed. Which should we use: words or syllables? It seems inevitable that when we think of the content of the message contained in an intonation unit, we shall refer to words. However, strictly speaking, an intonation unit is a structure of sound and belongs to phonology.

Halliday (and others[2]) show how intonation belongs to phonology. There is a hierarchy of phonological structures and units. It can be described in the following way: an intonation unit has a structure (is made up) of one or more rhythmic units, or 'feet'; each foot has a structure of syllables; and each syllable has a structure of phonemes. Thus there are four ranks of phonological structure: at the lowest level, phonemes, then syllables, feet and intonation units.

It can also be shown that there is a relationship of function, as well as structure, between the ranks. Certain phonemes have certain functions in the syllable: vowels, in the main, function as the nuclei of syllables, consonants as the margins. Then, certain types of syllable have their functions in feet (rhythmic units): stressed syllables function as the nuclei of feet, unstressed syllables as margins. And certain types of feet have their function in intonation units: the foot containing the tonic acts as the nucleus, the others contribute to the head and the tail. The nucleus at each rank is obligatory; the rest of the structure may or may not be present. It seems inevitable, therefore, that when we think of the formal structure of the intonation unit, we shall use phonological terms like 'feet' and their structure of stressed and unstressed 'syllables'. The labels and examples of Table 1.2 can thus be interpreted in terms of words or syllables, depending on whether we are dealing with meaning or form, respectively.

But what if the tonic consists of a word with more than one syllable, as in (1.14)?

(1.14)   'Snakes are 'men's 'most 'dangerous 'enemies

The most prominent word, *enemies*, is the tonic segment; the stressed initial syllable is the tonic syllable and the subsequent unstressed syllables are the tail. In (1.15), the prominent word gets divided even further.

(1.15)   But 'that's 'quite ri'diculous

The prominent word is *ridiculous*: the stressed syllable is -*dic*-; the following syllables constitute the tail, but the initial, unstressed, syllable belongs intonationally to the head.

We have now considered all parts of the structure of an intonation unit. The tonic (or nucleus) is obligatory; without it we cannot identify a complete unit. The head, pre-head and tail are optional in the sense that they may or may not be present. It should also be remembered that we identify these components solely on the grounds that they are points, or areas, where meaning can be affected by variations in an intonation pattern. It should now be possible for you to identify the four components in each of the examples listed from (1.5) to (1.9); remember that (1.7) and (1.9) comprise two separate units each.[3]

The fact that intonation units display structure (as well as system) should help to dispel the notion that intonation is so nebulous and subjective a phenomenon that it defies analysis and description. Because the structure of intonation units can be identified and described, it should now be possible to view intonation as a phenomenon that can not only be analysed, but taught, understood and learnt. Furthermore, the intonation system and structure of one language can be compared and contrasted with those of another.

4. Functions

We turn now to the uses we make of intonation. System and structure relate to the **nature** of intonation: what intonation is like. We turn now to what intonation does: its **functions**.

Some of its functions have already been alluded to, and here we will briefly introduce and illustrate its six major functions.

4.1 The organization of information

Perhaps the most important, and least appreciated, function of intonation is to present the management of information as the speaker perceives it. In a typical conversation a person knows the information they want to present, but then has to present it in pieces that are manageable not only to themselves but also to the people they are addressing. We saw a snippet of conversation in (1.3) above. It was simply too much information to present in a single unit, and the speaker had to divide it up and present it a piece at a time. The main topic is presented first:[4]

(1.3a)   I regret + putting the <u>people</u> out of the out of the South Side and central Edinburgh

and is followed up immediately with an appeal to his addressee to believe him:

(1.3b)   you <u>know</u>

He then starts, but abandons, a new idea; he is obviously still trying to sort out in his mind how he might best present his ideas:

(1.3c)   ++ I don't think

He now restarts, having decided to set out first of all a reference to the past:

(1.3d)   ++ especially after the war you know

(Incidentally, the *you know* of (1.3d) is not made as prominent as that of (1.3b) was; hence it does not constitute a separate intonation unit in (1.3d).)

As he fumbles in his mind for the words he needs, he repeats the time reference and proceeds:

(1.3e)   after the ++ war when they started the ++ redevelopment

16

The pause before *redevelopment* suggests a difficulty in deciding upon the word, but he cannot think of the next word and so abandons the next unit:

(1.3f)   and the

(1.3g)   ++ well the authority more or less <u>made</u> it

and follows up with the next point:

(1.3h)   that everybody was to go out<u>side</u>

and an appeal as in (1.3b)

(1.3i)   you <u>know</u>

and another new point:

(1.3j)   ++ the gardens and <u>houses</u>

The organization of information involves decisions about the division of information into manageable pieces and their 'staging' – what comes first, what follows, what precedes, and so on. It also involves grading the pieces of information into major and minor and tying them up into coherent sequences. The division and staging are handled by tonality, with boundaries of intonation units; and the grading is handled by tone: rises, falls, and fall-rises.

There is also another important aspect to the organization of information, and that is the decision as to what should be made prominent in any piece of information. This is usually discussed in terms of 'new' and 'given' (or 'old') information, and is neatly illustrated in (1.3). You will notice that in (1.3a) the word *people* is more prominent than either *South Side* or *central Edinburgh*. What is left non-prominent, especially after the tonic, is considered by the speaker as 'given' information, i.e. it has been mentioned or alluded to before, or is being treated as common knowledge or as obvious in the current situation. Thus what is 'new' in (1.3a) is *people*, and we must assume that the locations have been mentioned before – either by the speaker or someone else participating in the conversation.

In (1.3d) the word *war* is prominent; it is new. But in (1.3e), it is not prominent and is treated, understandably, as given.

This information structure within the intonation unit is handled by tonicity: the location of the tonic.

Not all spoken discourse is as unfluent as the snippet of conversation that we have been analysing. Spoken discourse which has been rehearsed, e.g. newsreading, story-telling, joke-telling, teaching, preaching, etc. is likely to be much more fluent, but whether the discourse is executed fluently or not, it will still be subject to the speaker's management of the information. The type (or 'genre') of spoken discourse is immaterial in this connection: decisions must be made by the speaker in every discourse with respect to the division and staging of information (tonality), the structure of new and given information within each unit (tonicity) and the grading of one piece of information against another (tone).

This function of intonation, the organization of information, seems to be a basic function, so basic, in fact, that people are hardly conscious of it.

4.2 The realization of communicative functions

Another basic function of intonation is to present the speaker's purpose in saying something; whether the speaker is telling you something, asking you, ordering you, pleading with you, or just plainly greeting you or thanking you, etc. This dimension to talk has commonly been labelled the 'communicative function' by the language teaching profession; philosophers and linguists also call this dimension 'discourse function', 'speech functions', 'speech acts' and 'illocution'. They all refer to the intended effect that the speaker wishes to produce on those who are being addressed. Whereas the informational function of intonation answers the question 'What is being said?', the communicative or illocutionary function addresses the question 'Why is it being said?'

We have already alluded to this function also, in example (1.2), when we discussed the different effects that a falling pitch and a rising pitch have on the tag *isn't he*:

(1.2)   (John's going out), i̲s̲n't he

The fall suggests certainty, 'knowing'; the rise suggests uncertainty, 'querying'. Generally speaking, a falling tone in an intonation unit that contains major information denotes 'speaker-dominance': the speaker knows and tells, orders, demands, etc. On the other hand, a rising tone in an equivalent unit denotes 'speaker-deference': the speaker does not know and so asks, does not have authority and so requests, coaxes, etc. Let us illustrate further.

If you feel you are in the privileged position of authority and expect to be able to tell people to do something, you might well say (1.16):

(1.16)   Shut the wi̲n̲dow

with a falling tone. On the other hand, if you do not feel you are in such a privileged position, you might resort to a request rather than an order; in which case, you could still use (1.16), but with a rise. Try the two versions; for the request, it is important to pitch the word *Shut* reasonably high, the word *the* lower, and the first syllable of *window* lower again; the rise then begins with the low pitch of *win-* and continues upwards in *-dow*. Notice, again, that the difference of communicative function is realized solely through intonation; the wording of (1.16) remains constant.

Admittedly, if you are making a request, you might well append a politeness word like *please*. But notice that even with this addition, the request is going to have a rising tone:

(1.16a)   Shut the <u>win</u>dow, please

The rise that is begun on the tonic syllable continues upwards right through the tail (-*dow, please*). The fact that the request can be either with or without the word *please*, shows that it is the intonation that is the principal means of realizing the request function, not just the word *please*.

Here is another example of contrasting communicative functions. (1.17) would be interpreted as an exclamation if it was accompanied by a falling tone:

(1.17)   Isn't it <u>hot</u>

It is typically used to comment on unexpectedly hot weather and is frequently prefaced with an exclamatory gesture like *phew!* But you will have no difficulty in thinking of other situations where the degree of hotness might have been unexpected; think, for instance, of the astonishment somebody might show when the value of a microwave oven is being demonstrated to show how quickly food can be made very hot.

Now, on the other hand, think of what the microwave oven demonstrator might say when he or she offers heated food when the oven has been inadvertently left on defrost; the other person expects hot food, but is disappointed and protests. The demonstrator, temporarily mystified, is quite likely to say (1.17) with a rise on *hot* as a genuine question.

Try the two versions of it; for the rising version, try to keep *Isn't it* quite high, and start the rise on *hot* at a low pitch and raise the pitch as you say the word. A slightly different rendering of the rising tone may well occur to you, too: starting the rise on *Is-* and continuing upwards through -*n't it hot*, as (1.17a):

(1.17a)   <u>Is</u>n't it hot

It is still a question, but seems to add an element of surprise or puzzlement. (Notice that *hot* is no longer the prominent word; 'hotness' is now being taken for granted; it is being treated as 'given'. *Isn't* is prominent instead, in contrast to the imagined *It is* of expectation.)

To return to the main theme, falls and rises indicate, in broad terms, the communicative intent of the speaker. Thus intonation can distinguish between statements and queries, orders and requests, exclamations and questions, and the like, even when the actual wording remains constant. This communicative function of intonation is a basic function of intonation too, because whenever we say something, we have a purpose in doing so.

4.3 The expression of attitude

This third function is probably the most familiar, and it was certainly considered as the primary function in the older, more traditional, studies of intonation. It corresponds most clearly to the observation 'Not what they said, but the way they said it'. The 'way they said it' usually refers to the mood of the speaker or the attitude shown to the addressee or the message. A message, a piece of information, can be given politely, grumpily, angrily, warmly and so on.

But a message can also be given without any particular emotion, as a plain piece of information, as is typical in newsreading. We can simply pass on a piece of information, or ask for information without an overlay of emotion; such a style is labelled either 'plain' or 'neutral'. This is a useful concept, because we can then define the expression of attitude as departures from neutral patterns of intonation. This function answers the question 'How is it being said?'

Intonation, however, is not the only means available to a speaker to convey attitudes. First of all, there is the wider range of vocal effects and paralinguistic features mentioned above: voice qualities, vocal effects (like sighing, sniggering or humming), tempo and loudness. Secondly, there are gestures of the face, hands and body; distance and proximity, eye contact or the lack of it, also indicate kinds of relationship between speaker and addressee and thus convey attitude. Thirdly, the choice of words can be an indication of attitude; there are angry words like *stupid*, affectionate words, swear words; words can be chosen to have a sarcastic effect or to flatter, and so on.[5]

If you are angry, you will **sound** angry and employ appropriate gestures and words and a range of paralinguistic features; but the sound of anger will also be expressed in pitch - quite typically in a high pitch sustained throughout the utterance, such as in (1.18).

(1.18)   You stupid <u>fool</u> | Look what you've been and <u>done</u>

The effect of attitude is mainly to be found in the extent of a fall or rise and in variations of pitch in the head and pre-head. A wide falling tone (falling from a higher pitch than normal, to low), for instance, usually denotes surprise, intensity, something unexpected; a narrow falling tone (falling from lower than normal, to low), on the other hand, denotes mildness, something expected. Try (1.19) with a normal, neutral fall on *again*, to represent a plain statement; then with a wide fall, from high to low, to represent surprise, enthusiasm, unexpectedness; and then with a narrow fall, from mid-low to low, to represent expectedness, or even lack of interest:

(1.19)   The Conservatives won a<u>gain</u>

Your preferred intonation will indicate your attitude to the message. Notice, again, that intonation can indicate a variety of attitudes without a change of wording; in such cases, it becomes clear that intonation has been solely responsible for the expression of attitude.

4.4 Syntactic structure

The fourth function relates intonation to the syntax of clauses. In English, there are many cases where two syntactic patterns can only be distinguished by intonation. One example has already been given: the distinction between defining (or 'restrictive') relative clauses as in (1.8):

(1.8)   My brother who lives in Nai<u>ro</u>bi

and non-defining (or 'non-restrictive') relative clauses in (1.9):

(1.9)   My brother | who lives in Nai<u>ro</u>bi

The non-defining relative clauses like (1.9) have, incidentally, also been called 'adding clauses', which perhaps more clearly indicates their function.[6] The grammatical distinction between (1.8) and (1.9) plainly represents a choice of meaning, which is overtly signalled by intonation in its spoken form. (In its written form, a comma would be expected after *brother* in (1.9), but since writers are notoriously inconsistent in their use of commas, there is no guarantee that the distinction would be signalled in writing. In speech, the signal is obligatory.) The parallel wording of the two structures is disambiguated in speech.

Another frequently cited example is the parallel wording of two clause types as in (1.20) and (1.21):

(1.20)   She washed and brushed her <u>hair</u>

(1.21)   She <u>washed</u> | and brushed her <u>hair</u>

In (1.20), *hair* is deemed to be the direct object complementing both *washed* and *brushed*; thus *washed* (and *brushed*) is transitive. In (1.21), however, with an intonation unit boundary immediately after *washed*, the word *hair* is deemed to be the direct object complementing *brushed* only, thus leaving *washed* as intransitive – in the sense of simply washing oneself, presumably only hands and face (but not hair!). So (1.21) means that the person washed herself (but presumably *not* her hair) and then did something about her hair. Intonation has thus made the distinction between a transitive (1.20) and an intransitive (1.21) use of the verb *wash*, despite the identical wording.

You may be able to think of other possible examples: look for verbs that can be either transitive or intransitive and concoct a pair of sentences on the model of (1.20) and (1.21). Take for example a verb like *dress, hide, teach,* etc.; work out two meanings parallel to (1.20) and (1.21), e.g. *She dressed and fed the baby.* (Again, it must be conceded that commas might well be used to disambiguate these cases, but commas are part of the written mode of English; in the spoken mode, we depend on intonation.)

It might also be argued that the equivalent in other languages (like German, Dutch, French, Italian, etc.) would require the reflexive pronoun in cases like (1.21); indeed, you could add *herself* to the English version. But two points can be made in this connection: first, the English version without *herself* is perfectly normal, and possibly more frequent, and English speakers are quite content to rely on the intonation to provide the sense; second, what may be true of another language does not impinge on the linguistic description of English. What is true of German will be incorporated into the description of German, not into the description of English or any other language. Similarly, what is true of English may, or may not, be parallel to what is true of German, or any other language.

There are many more cases of two grammatical structures being disambiguated by intonation in the spoken form of English, and these will be dealt with in the course of Chapter 2. But the case of the reflexive pronoun is also involved in a different kind of grammatical structure. Also, the two illustrations of grammatical contrast so far involve tonality: one intonation unit in (1.8) and (1.20), but two in the parallel wordings of (1.9) and (1.21). In (1.22) and (1.23) the grammatical contrast is apparent in the tonicity:

(1.22)   He <u>asked</u> himself

(1.23)   He asked him<u>self</u>

In (1.22), *himself* is a reflexive pronoun functioning as the direct object complementing *asked*; thus *asked* is transitive, and *himself* is reflexive. In (1.23), however, it is an emphatic pronoun; (1.23) means that he himself did the asking, he did not leave the asking to anybody else. Thus, in (1.23), *asked* is intransitive, and *himself* is emphatic. Admittedly, it could be argued that (1.23) can be expressed differently as *He himself asked*; but the wording of (1.23) is perfectly normal, and possibly more frequent, and English speakers are quite content to rely on the intonation to provide the sense. (Could the written forms be distinguished to provide the sense in this case?)

Again, you may be able to think of other possible examples; look for verbs that can be either transitive or intransitive and in their intransitive use could be reasonably followed by an emphatic pronoun. I recall an occasion when the hostess at a party was asked while she was in the kitchen if the guests could begin on the (as yet uncut) cake; since she was not in a position to cut the cake herself, she called out:

(1.24)   Cut your<u>self</u>

i.e. you do the cutting. The alternative, with tonic on *Cut*, was most definitely not intended!

Intonation has a grammatical role in disambiguating parallel wordings of different syntactic structures. Whereas the first three functions of intonation that we have discussed would be common to all languages (in general terms, though not in details), this grammatical function may not be so. It is quite likely that another language would employ overtly grammatical means to differentiate between all its grammatical systems and not rely on intonation. English, however, does use intonation for this purpose.

4.5 Textual structure

The fifth major function of intonation concerns longer structures than single units of intonation and individual pieces of information. Obviously, an intonation unit and a piece of information do not usually appear in isolation. We have dealt with them in isolation for the most part in order to illustrate the informational, communicative, attitudinal and grammatical functions without any distracting complication. But we have already examined a bit of larger text in (1.3) with its eight complete units and two abandoned units. The units did not appear in isolation but in combination with each other as part of the staging in the management of the message. How do these separate, discrete, units of intonation hang together to form the text of discourse?

Naturally, the topic of the message is one factor that binds the information together; another is the grammatical systems of reference and conjunction that show that clauses and sentences belong together; and a third factor is intonation.

To illustrate how intonation performs this function, think first of all of how you know when one item of news has finished and a new one begins, in newsreading. No one tells you, but you know. A new item usually starts on a fairly high pitch: the first onset syllable is high and the general pitch level of the whole of that intonation unit is relatively high. When that item comes to an end, the general pitch level of its final intonation unit is relatively low, the tone will fall to its lowest pitch and there is often a slackening of pace in the final few words. A noticeable pause signals the end of that item. Then comes the next item, and the first onset syllable of the initial intonation unit of the new item is high and then comes a gradual descent in the general pitch level of the following units until the lowest point is reached with the final unit. This pattern of high start, gradual descent and low finish is typical of newsreading and is detectable in other spoken genres, especially where the discourse has been rehearsed or the semantic content prepared, as in the telling of stories and jokes. The combination of pitch descent and pause serves to combine units together but serves also to detach the final unit of one item from the initial unit of the next.

This phenomenon has been called phonological paragraphing. It should not come as too much of a surprise that there is an equivalent paragraph structure in spoken discourse to that found in the written mode. Paragraphs in writing usually indicate the division of the larger text into separate smaller topics. The same kind of division is, not unnaturally, found in spoken discourse too. The intonation pattern described above is thus the equivalent of starting a new paragraph on a new line. (Brown (1977) coined the term 'para*tone*' in contrast to 'para*graph*'.[7])

The key to phonological paragraphs is:

(1) The high pitch on the onset syllable of the initial intonation unit.

(2) The relatively high 'baseline' of that initial unit; this means that the low pitches are relatively high, compared to the low pitches in the final unit of the paragraph.

(3) There is a gradual lowering of that baseline until the final unit is reached.

(4) The depth of fall in the final unit is the lowest in the whole paragraph.

(5) There is usually a slowing down process in the final unit.[8]

(6) There is a longer pause than is normally allowed between intonation units.

```
200
150
100
I   regret  +   putting  the people  out  of  the  out  of   the   South     Side     and   central   Edinburgh you
155 200          150      115 190    160 120 115 120 105  105  120-105  120-105  110  120-115   120-100  105
```

```
know  ++ 0.86    I   don't  think ++ 1.8     especially   after    the  war  you know after  the ++ 0.64
140.100          145 175    100             165-115     140-110   150  110 120  150    100
```

```
war  when they  started  the ++ 0.32  redevelopment    and   the ++ 1.00   well  the  authority  more  or  less
120  120   100  130-100  100         105-120-100-120   100   110           120   135  165-100    120      100
```

```
made  it  that  everybody was to  go  outside you  know   ++ 0.68 the  gardens  and  houses  but
140   100       125-100  100 100 100 130-95    130-100          90  130-110  100  120-90  120
```

Figure 1.1 A visual display of the information of extract (1.3). Original information retained from Brown, Currie and Kenworthy (1980: 66) on prominence (i.e. underlined syllables) and frequencies

Listen to the news and see if you can identify these six factors. You should also be able to detect them in story-telling, and even in jokes. It is also possible to find them in the more unfluent, spontaneous discourse of informal conversation, although not so clearly. Figure 1.1 is a visual display of the snippet of conversation (1.3) that we have examined before on a couple of occasions; you will notice how high the initial onset syllable in *regret* is pronounced in the initial unit of this paragraph; that *don't* is slightly lower; *especially* lower again and *war* even lower; then *authority* is high again, as the beginning of the new topic.

Brazil, Coulthard and Johns (1980) also provided specimens of recorded text. Here is part of their Transcript A, arranged in phonological paragraphs and with a simplified transcription: H = high baseline (or 'key'); M = mid baseline; L = low baseline. A teacher is addressing his class in the middle of a lesson and wishes to introduce the subject of energy.

(1.25)

H	'Put your <u>pens</u>			
M		'down	'<u>Pencils</u>	
L				'down ‖

H	'<u>Now</u> |be'fore I came to
M	'school	
L	'this '<u>morning</u>	

H	I had some '<u>cereal</u>	
M	
L	I 'had my '<u>breakfast</u> ‖

H	
M	and I had some '<u>toast</u>	and I had an '<u>egg</u>	and
L	

H	
M	I had a cup of '<u>tea</u>	and I had a '<u>biscuit</u>	
L	

H	
M	and <u>then</u> I came to
L	<u>school</u> ‖

The first phonological paragraph simply consists of two intonation units, and you see the progression from high to low. (The teacher actually followed this up with a few more similar instructions to obtain the pupils' attention.) Then comes another paragraph which gives an outline of the immediate topic, with a clear progression from high to low. The final unit of that paragraph is immediately followed by a unit on a high baseline, and so you can recognize that a new paragraph has been initiated. This third paragraph carries on with a number of mid-baseline units before a low one is reached; this is one way of extending the length of a phonological paragraph.

This system of gradually lowering the baseline in successive intonation units is an effective way of indicating that the units belong together. But this system can be interrupted to produce other effects. If a following unit is pronounced on a higher baseline, against the expectation of a lower one, the effect produced is one of contrast or surprise:

(1.26)   H   'Wales played   'beat them 'one 'nil
          M   Bra'zil | and
          L

If a following unit is pitched on the same baseline as the previous one, it usually means that the second unit is deemed to be an addition to the first, and that could be the interpretation of the sequence of mid-baseline units in the example above, referring to items taken for breakfast.

If a following unit suffers a sudden drop in pitch, that has the effect of indicating that the information was deemed to be fully expected:

(1.27)   H   The 'Monster 'Raving 'Loony 'Party's 'candidate |
          M
          L   'lost his deposit

You will no doubt have noticed how the pitch variations in these sequences of intonation units match the attitudinal function in individual units: high for unexpected, mid for neutral, low for fully expected.[9]

However, there is a familiar, additional, meaning for low-pitched units embedded in a higher-pitched context, namely asides, glosses, and the like:

(1.28)   H   And 'then he ac'cused me |
          M
          L   I don't know 'where
          H   of 'stealing ||
          M
          L   he got the i'dea from |

(1.29)   H   But then the 'next 'student |
          M
          L   a 'really 'clever 'bloke |
          H   got 'everything 'right ||
          M
          L

(1.30)   H   He's 'coming |
          M   to'night ||
          L   he 'said |

4.6 The identification of speech styles

The final major function of intonation that we need to consider is its role in the way in which we can identify different speech styles, or 'genres'. People engage in a very wide range of differing language events; informal conversation is one type of language event and is very different from other types of dialogue like interviews, debates, interrogations, air-to-ground communication by pilots, and so on. Monologues vary considerably too; compare, for example, newsreading and prayer, or story-telling and poetry reading, or a comedian's monologue and a lecture!

If you switch the radio on (or the television before the screen clarifies), you can usually tell within seconds what kind of language event is taking place. This is because newsreading, for example, somehow sounds different from all other styles. We probably differentiate dozens of different styles simply on the basis of the general sound of even just a few seconds of spoken discourse. And we can usually manage this even if the actual words are muffled, as they might be, say, in an adjoining room. There is something about the general sound of particular language events that identifies them.

This general sound of a particular language event is known as its prosodic composition. Differences in prosodic composition depend on a number of features: degree of formality, number of participants, degree of privacy, degree of semantic preparation, and whether the spoken discourse was scripted or not. These features register in intonation, loudness, tempo, rhythmicality, paralinguistic features and hesitation pauses. Rhythmicality refers to degrees of rhythmic regularity, ranging from very regular, as in poetry reading and prayer in unison (e.g. the Lord's Prayer, said in public), to irregular, as in informal, unfluent, conversation.

As far as intonation in particular is concerned, styles vary in the proportions of falls and rises, relative length of intonation units and degree of textual structure (phonological paragraphing). Prayer, noticeably, manages without tone variation as a rule; tonic syllables are held level and it is usually only the *Amen* that has a falling tone.

The fullest study to date on the prosodic composition of speech styles[10] compared the following genres:

(i) informal conversations (private, unscripted)

(ii) informal narration of an anecdote (private, unscripted)

(iii) a news bulletin (public, scripted)

(iv) Bible reading in church (public, scripted)

(v) individual prayer (public, unscripted)

(vi) prayer in unison (public, scripted, but uttered by a body of people simultaneously)

The prosodic composition of these six genres is displayed in Table 1.3:

	Informal conversation	Anecdote	News-reading	Bible reading	Individual prayer	Prayer in unison
paragraphing		Yes	Yes	Yes		
punctuation group	n/a	n/a	Yes	Yes	n/a	Yes
short units	Yes			Yes	Yes	Yes
tone variation	Yes	Yes	Yes	Yes		
high proportion of falls	Yes					
high proportion of pre-tonic variation			Yes	Yes		
forte				Yes	Yes	
lento				Yes	Yes	Yes
rhythmic				Yes	Yes	Yes
paralinguistic features	Yes	Yes		Yes	Yes	
hesitation	Yes	Yes			Yes	

TABLE 1.3 The prosodic composition of different genres

A few points emerge. The recognition of phonological paragraphs is most apparent in semantically-prepared discourse. It is not that it is impossible to find paragraphs in other styles, but in semantically-prepared discourse it is at its clearest. Secondly, intonation unit boundaries correspond to punctuation in scripted discourse. Thirdly, the intonation units themselves tend to be longer in semantically-prepared discourse, except where the delivery style is fairly slow ('lento') and loud ('forte'); units are generally shorter in informal conversation when the message is being composed and relayed almost simultaneously. Fourthly, there is a high proportion of falls in informal conversation; this means that there are more individual, major, pieces of information in that genre than, for instance, in narrating an anecdote or in newsreading; in the latter styles, the speaker has a much stronger sense of linking incomplete pieces of information with complete (see Chapter 4). Fifthly, and possibly surprisingly, public, scripted, spoken discourse is characterized by greater pitch variation in the pre-tonic segment; this variation, no doubt, is intended to relieve any impression of dull, routine repetition that could bore the hearers. Sixthly, newsreading eschews paralinguistic features altogether: the newsreaders' feelings are not allowed, in the main, to intrude into the news. Prayer in unison shares this lack of paralanguage, for the simple reason that a body of people simultaneously engaged in speech do not have the opportunity to introduce their own feelings. Finally, and expectedly, hesitation features in those genres that are unscripted, even if a degree of semantic preparation has taken place.

Thus, it can be seen that intonation is a major identifying factor in the prosodic composition of different genres of spoken discourse. This particular function operates on a much larger body of discourse than the other functions, but it is nevertheless recognizable.

5. Conclusion

We have just considered six major functions of intonation in English. All of them, except possibly the grammatical function, will manifest themselves in all languages. A seventh function might occur to you, and indeed was alluded to on the first page: a sociolinguistic function, in describing, comparing and contrasting one accent (or dialect) with another. Such a function relates to the **user** rather than the **use** of language, and on that score will not be considered further in this book, interesting though such a subject is. However, you cannot describe, compare and contrast the intonation system of two accents until you have a basic framework for the description of one. That is what this book will seek to provide.

Similarly, intonation can function in psycholinguistics, too. The intonation of baby speech is quite different from children's and adult speech. The sociolinguistic and psycholinguistic aspects of intonation study have been labelled the 'indexical function'[11] in the sense that they identify characteristics of the speaker rather than of the message and the discourse. Research into the indexical functions of intonation and indeed into the genre and textual functioning is still at a relatively elementary stage and will not feature significantly in this book.

This book will concentrate on presenting the body of knowledge that has been established on the functions of intonation in conveying the meaning of messages:

what is being said (information)

why it is being said (communicative functions)

how it is being said (attitudes)

which is being said (grammar; differentiation between syntactic choices)

It will deal with the structure and phonetic details of English intonation as they form part of the three systems of tonality, tonicity and tone.

Notes

1. See, for example, Roach (1983: 121).

2. See Halliday (1967), Pike (1967) and Tench (1990).

3.

(1.5)	head		tonic	tail		
	'What are you 'going to		<u>do</u>	tonight		
(1.6)	pre-head	head	tonic	tail		
	I'm	'going into	<u>'town</u>	this 'morning		
(1.7)	pre-head	head	tonic	pre-head	tonic	tail
	I'm	'going into	<u>'town</u>	this	<u>'morn</u>	ing

(1.8)	pre-head	head			tonic	tail
	My	'brother who 'lives in Nai			'ro	bi

(1.9)	pre-head	tonic	tail	pre-head	head		tonic	tail
	My	'bro	ther	who	'lives in Nai		'ro	bi

4. See the analysis of this snippet of conversation in Tench (1990: 181f.).

5. For a fuller discussion, see Tench (1990: 392–8; 440–6).

6. See Sinclair (1972) and Young (1980).

7. Brazil and Coulthard (1979) used the term 'pitch sequences' and demonstrated that this kind of textual structuring exists not only in monologue but in dialogue, too.

8. Lehiste (1975, 1979) refers to this as 'pre-boundary lengthening'.

9. See Brazil, Coulthard and Johns (1980: chapter 2) for a fuller discussion of this system which they call 'key'.

10. See Tench (1990: chapter 7; also 1988). See also Crystal and Davy (1975) for further details of the characteristics of informal conversation, and Johns-Lewis (1986) for a comparison of conversation with acting and reading aloud.

11. See Couper-Kuhlen (1986).

2

Tonality

THE UNITS OF INTONATION

---

1. Neutral tonality

Tonality is the system in intonation that divides spoken discourse into its separate individual intonation units. Spoken discourse sometimes consists of only one message or piece of information; indeed it might consist of only one word, even only one syllable, e.g. *Yes, No, Right, So?*, etc. But it usually consists of more than one piece of information, and often extends for as much as an hour, or more, either as a monologue or as a series of turns in a dialogue. The whole text is composed of many intonation units, each bearing a single piece of information and representing the speaker's management of the information of the whole message. To give some idea of quantities, a two-minute news bulletin has usually between 70 and 80 intonation units; admittedly, the pace at which they are delivered is fast in newsreading, but even in relaxed informal speech, there would be approximately 25 units per minute.

Each intonation unit contains one piece of information - as the speaker perceives it. It is important to emphasize the perception and management of the organization of information by **the speaker**. It is very easy to look at the transcript of a record of speech and think you would have organized it differently from the original speaker. You could well be right and if you had had to give the same message using the same words you might well have divided the material differently: but **your** division (or segmentation) represents **your** perception, whereas the tonality of the original represented that person's perception. (It is a recurring problem when introducing intonation to get people to concentrate on one particular issue in intonation, when they can think of many alternative renderings!)

Halliday also drew attention to the observation that very often intonation units coincide with clauses, and this provides a very valuable starting-point for the description of tonality. If a person wants to give a piece of

31

information, it is conveyed as a single unit of intonation, but it has to be worded, and this is where grammar comes in. The clause is the most obvious unit of grammar to handle a typical piece of information: the subject represents the theme – what the message is about; the predicate represents the rheme – what the message actually is. For instance, the syntax of

(1.10)   A dog is a man's best friend

tells you what the theme is, i.e. the subject of the clause, *a dog*; and then tells you what the actual message is, i.e. the predicate, *is a man's best friend* (the 'rheme').

It should be noted, however, that this coincidence of tonality and clause is by no means a hard and fast rule. However, in Halliday's words (1967: 18–19), there is a

> tendency for the tone group[1] to correspond in extent with the clause; we may take advantage of this tendency by regarding the selection of one complete tone group for one complete clause as the neutral term ... That is to say, a clause that consists of one and only one tone group will be regarded as 'neutral in tonality'.

It is useful theoretically to lay a foundation for tonality on this basis: that a single piece of information is handled in the grammar typically by a single clause, and in pronunciation by a single intonation unit.

It must also be emphasized that this is not a case of squeezing facts into ready made theories. In one count,[2] 916 intonation units, out of a total of 1,880 in the whole data, corresponded to complete clauses – almost 50 per cent. And here is part of the transcript of a conversation between two women on the subject of Bonfire Night, recorded by Crystal and Davy (1975); note the frequency with which intonation units embrace the main elements of the clause: there are nine clauses in the first eighteen completed intonation units.

(2.1)   A: we're 'looking 'forward to \bon<u>fire</u> night
              at \<u>least</u>
              the ∨ <u>child</u>ren 'are
              - - do you in\<u>dulge</u> in 'this -
        B: oh in . in ∨ <u>sus</u>sex we 'did
              - - I've - in \<u>fact</u>
              I 'went to 'one 'last ˋ<u>week</u>
              . but . it was .
        A: xxx
              'that was a bit /<u>ear</u>ly
              ⁄<u>was</u>n't it

B: 'all the 'all the `joys were
    `joy
    was 'taken <u>out</u> of it
    for ⁄<u>me</u>
    be'cause it was – a `<u>huge</u>
    . \<u>bonfire</u>
    in a 'garden the 'size of this ∨ <u>room</u>
    - with 'big \<u>houses</u>
    'all a\<u>round</u>
    - and the 'bonfire was 'right `<u>under</u>
    with its 'leaves ∧ <u>all</u> 'dry

The concept of neutral tonality is a very useful starting-point. It embraces a very important point: the functional equivalence of intonation unit, clause and unit of information, linking up phonology with grammar and semantics. Furthermore, this functional equivalence is realized to a large extent in actual discourse.

Here is another text from Crystal and Davy (1975: 44) without the intonation marks. See if you can guess what the intonation units would be; mark the boundaries with a | ; a dot represents a very brief pause; a hyphen, or hyphens, relatively larger pauses; bracketed words represent the listener's back channel.

(2.2)   yes I remember there was a terrible story – horrifying story that was told by a colleague of mine when I used to teach years ago – who erm . this chap lived in erm a – a semi deta . detached house and next door there was . a man who'd just bought a new car – and he was telling me that one morning he was looking through the window – and this . man allowed his wife to drive the car very unwisely and she was having a first go in it – (m) . and – he backed it out of the garage – so that it was standing on the driveway . and he'd closed the garage doors – (yeah) . and – she came out of the house to . take this car out and go shopping for the first time – so she came out very gingerly – and opened the door . and sat in the car – and – er . began to back . very very gently – taking great care you see that she didn't do anything to this . to this new car – and –– as she backed – there was an unpleasant . crunching sound (*laughs*) and she slapped on the brakes and looked around frantically – and realized that she hadn't opened the . gates . that . let on to the main road you see (oh) . and she'd just backed into these

In my experience, a group of people doing the same exercise would show a degree of conformity of about 80 per cent. But why wouldn't they all agree in the whole passage? There are two main reasons for individual diversity: one is the imagined speed of delivery: the slower the pace, the shorter the unit; and the second is exactly what we discussed above: people's perception of the organization of information will vary.

2. Marked tonality

We must now try to account for all those cases where intonation units do not coincide with whole clauses. Marked tonality, i.e. any case that does not correspond to neutral tonality, occurs either when two (or more) clauses fit into a single intonation unit, or when – and this is much more frequently the case – two (or more) intonation units are needed to cover a single clause.

The most obvious case is when a speaker presents two (or more) pieces of information in a single clause as in (1.7):

(1.7)   I'm going to town | this morning

Quite possibly, *this morning* is added as an afterthought, as we mentioned in Chapter 1. Examples can be found in the bonfire text: *with big houses | all around*, two units added as afterthoughts to an already long clause.

On the other hand, two clauses may fit into a single intonation unit, as we saw in the case of (1.4):

(1.4)   He did. I saw it.

He did, in this case, is said quite quickly, as 'given' information; the new information is contained in the second clause (or sentence, in this case). A different case occurs where two verbs share the same complementing object, as in (1.20); strictly speaking, that sequence constitutes two clauses. Similarly, the verbs *come, go, try* and *stop* frequently precede another verb in combinations like *come and see, go and look for it, try and stop me, stop and think*.

Two other, odd, cases could be mentioned here too, since they might look like tonality contrasts. You could say the following words, *He spoke to me honestly*, as a single clause and in a single intonation unit:

(2.3)   He spoke to me <u>hon</u>estly

Or, you could treat *honestly* as a separate unit:

(2.4)   He spoke to me | <u>hon</u>estly

in which case *honestly* is like an appeal to the addressee to believe the claim. (It might be written, in fact, as two sentences: *He spoke to me. Honestly!*) This distinction was once used in an advertisement:

HOW TO MAKE A FORTUNE
HONESTLY

By placing *honestly* on a separate line, the advertisers were able to exploit a feature of intonation successfully, since they knew that people would read the wording in two ways and thus they got two messages across in one advertisement.

Another similar example is the exploitation of two meanings of the word *so* in the following: *The reader will find them unusual and so puzzling. So* could be an intensifier like *very*:

(2.5)   The reader will find them un<u>u</u>sual | and so <u>puzz</u>ling

but *so* could be a substitution of a clause like *thus* or *consequently*, meaning, in this case, *because they are unusual (the reader will find them puzzling)*:

(2.6)   The reader will find them un<u>u</u>sual | and <u>so</u> | <u>puzz</u>ling

(If you know phonetic transcription, you might find an accidental clash between

(2.7)   aɪ dəʊnt nəʊ

and

(2.8)   aɪ 'dəʊnt | 'nəʊ

The first is a single clause; the second, a sequence of two.)

Other cases of marked tonality relate to the length and the structure of the clause concerned.

Intonation units have an average of between two and three feet each, i.e. two or three word stresses. Often, as we have seen, a unit might consist of only one stressed syllable. The usual **maximum** number of stresses in a unit is five, and this corresponds to the **maximum** number of elements in a single simple clause: subject, verb, direct object, indirect object and adjunct, e.g.:

(2.9)   'The children wrote 'postcards to their 'parents from 'camp

(2.10)   The 'office 'sends the 'students their 'grants in Oc'tober

This sentence could be said as one unit of intonation – and as one unit of information – but it reaches the maximum of five feet. If a clause breaches that maximum, it seems that it is automatically converted into two (or even more) intonation units: for example (2.11):

(2.11)   The 'train ar'riving at 'platform 'two | is the 'ten 'twenty from
         'Swansea to 'London 'Paddington

The tonality division depends on the structure of the clause. In (2.11), the subject is long enough to be separated off; in informational terms, the theme has been separated intonationally from the rheme, and this is very often the case. This is illustrated in the bonfire text (2.1):

'all the 'all the 'joys were 'joy | was 'taken 'out of it for 'me

The first unit is the theme, the second the rheme: this is clear despite the added complications of repetition and reformulation.

3. Lists

A list is a special kind of long clause. Each item is contained in a separate unit,[3] e.g.:

(2.12)   He could speak <u>Eng</u>lish | <u>French</u> | and <u>Ger</u>man

(2.13)   She ate some <u>soup</u> | some bread and <u>but</u>ter | and a piece of <u>cake</u>

Notice that *bread and butter* is treated in (2.13) as one list item; the speaker perceives it as one piece of information. However, in another context, *bread* and *butter* might be perceived as separate items, e.g.:

(2.14)   We need <u>milk</u> | some <u>bread</u> | and <u>but</u>ter

There is a potential for contrast here, as Halliday (1970: 36) has pointed out: compare (2.15) and (2.16):

(2.15)   We want <u>red</u> | <u>white</u> | and <u>blue</u> flags please

(2.16)   We want red white and <u>blue</u> flags please

(2.15) refers to three kinds of flags whereas (2.16) refers to one kind of flag with three colours. (2.16) is in fact an example of neutral tonality since the intonation unit contains the whole clause.

However (2.12), (2.13), (2.14) and (2.15) all display marked tonality since more than one unit was required for the list clause; each list item is treated as one piece of information, but they are all contained, grammatically, in one single clause.

Crystal (1969: 264) drew attention to a different kind of example involving idioms with *or*. *More or less* is an idiom that means 'just about', 'roughly', 'nearly'. Compare – talking of the potential punctuality, say, of a new train –

(2.17)   Will it be more or less on <u>time</u>?

and

(2.18)   Will it be <u>more</u> | or <u>less</u> on time?

The second case is rather like a list of two alternative possibilities. Similarly, *one or two* can be taken literally or as an idiom meaning 'some'.

Compare – when offering a warm drink –

(2.19)   Do you want one or two lumps of <u>su</u>gar?

and

(2.20)   Do you want <u>one</u> | or <u>two</u> lumps of sugar?

Where you have the extra tonality boundary, you have what amounts to a list.

———

4. Marked theme

Marked tonality is also occasioned by deviations to the structure of a clause. One deviation is to have a clause element preceding the subject with the effect that that element becomes the theme, instead of the subject, as in (2.21):

(2.21)   This morning | I'm going into town

The theme – the starting-point of the message – is no longer *I*, but *this morning*. This deviation is known as marked theme as opposed to the more usual, neutral, theme, in which the subject, coming first, is the theme; if anything (apart from conjunctions) precedes the subject, then that takes over the role of theme, it is the starting-point of the message.[4] Cases of such marked theme always have a separate intonation unit, and thus there are bound to be at least two units for such clauses. Consider these cases:

(2.22)   Last night | you came in too late

(2.23)   Whatever your excuse | you should be in by eleven

(2.24)   If you go out in the evening | I want you in by eleven

(2.22) and (2.23) are cases of marked theme producing marked tonality. (2.24), in fact, has a clause as marked theme, and is thus an example of neutral tonality, because each clause, the dependent one and the main one, has its own intonation unit.

Other typical cases of marked theme in a single clause are:

(2.25)   These ideas | you must reject

(2.26)   Not until then | will I even think about it

(2.27)   Scarcely even then | are you likely to find support

(2.28)   Into my mind | came the thought of rejecting it

5. Adjuncts

The other kind of structural deviation that affects tonality is the addition of certain kinds of adjunct either at the beginning or in the middle of a clause; these items generally have their own intonation unit. If these adjuncts appear at the end of the clause, they may either have an intonation unit of their own or be incorporated into the unit of the preceding clause; this choice of tonality, in the final position, affects tonicity also and so will be considered more fully in Chapter 3. Here, we will consider them in initial and medial positions, because in these positions they do affect tonality.

The adjuncts that affect tonality include linking adjuncts like *however, nevertheless, perhaps, of course, unfortunately*, etc. Consider (2.29) and (2.30):

(2.29)   Howe͟ver | he ran the mile in four mi͟nutes

(2.30)   He ran the mi͟le | howe͟ver | in four mi͟nutes

From the bonfire transcript (2.1) we have:

> at lea͟st | the chi͟ldren are
>
> in fa͟ct | I went to one last wee͟k

Also vocatives:

(2.31)   Miss Smi͟th | can you he͟lp me?

(2.32)   Can yo͟u | Miss Smi͟th | he͟lp me?

and viewpoint adjuncts like *politically, technically, from a personal point of view*, etc.:

(2.33)   Poli͟tically | the decision was a very cle͟ver one

(2.34)   The deci͟sion | from a poli͟tical point of view | was a very cle͟ver one.

6. Tags

Clauses may be concluded with a tag as in *it's hot, isn't it.* The tag has a particular form: it consists only of an operator and a subject pronoun, it is always in inverted order, and tense and number are determined by the main clause. Tags may be either positive or negative. If the polarity of the tag is reverse to that of the main clause – in other words, if negative follows positive, as in the above example, or positive follows negative, the tag is called a 'checking tag'. If the polarity of the tag follows that of the main clause – positive following positive (or, for some people, even negative following negative), then the tag is called a 'copy tag'.

The vast majority of tags have their own intonation unit. Example (1.2) should therefore be transcribed with the following tonality,

(1.2)   John's going ou͟t | i͟sn't he

An example occurred in the bonfire transcript (2.1):

> that was a bit ea͟rly | wa͟sn't it

Checking tags, i.e. those with reverse polarity, seem always to have separate intonation units for themselves, and certainly from the intonational point of view should, therefore, be regarded as separate clauses.[5] Thus, a tagged clause, viewed as a sequence of two clauses, follows the general rule of neutral tonality.

Copy tags, i.e. those with identical polarity, act somewhat differently. For one thing, copy tags can only be accompanied by a rising tone, whereas checking tags can be accompanied by either a falling or a rising tone, with a consequent change of meaning. You can check this for yourself: you can say (1.2) with either a rising or a falling tone on the tag, as you discovered in Chapter 1; but you can only say the tag of (2.35) with a rising tone:

(2.35)   John's going <u>out</u> | <u>is</u> he

If you try the *is he* with a falling tone, it will sound distinctly odd.

The second difference from checking tags, is that copy tags do not necessarily require their own, separate, intonation unit. You could say (2.35) with a falling tone on *out* and then keep the pitch of the voice low without allowing a rising tone:

(2.36)   John's going <u>out</u> is he

Notice that there is quite a difference in meaning between checking tags and copy tags. The use of checking tags implies an actual checking of the proposition in the main clause. the speaker is pretty certain of the validity of the proposition if the tone on the tag falls, whereas the speaker is less certain about the proposition and needs confirmation if the tone rises – in both cases, the proposition is being checked. The copy tag implies more of a realization – even a sudden realization – of the significance of the proposition; if there is no separate tonality for the copy tag, as in (2.36), there is added a note of irritation.

Work out all the meanings with a different example:

(2.37a)   They lost against \<u>New</u>port of all teams | /<u>did</u>n't they

(2.37b)   They lost against \<u>New</u>port of all teams | \<u>did</u>n't they

(2.37c)   They lost against \<u>New</u>port of all teams | /<u>did</u> they

(2.37d)   They lost against \<u>New</u>port of all teams did they

Try out these variations with examples of your own for (a) a degree of uncertainty, (b) certainty, (c) a (sudden) realization of the significance of the information, and (d) with a touch of irritation. Note that whereas (a), (b) and (c) have two intonation units, the tonality is different for (d).

7. Tonality contrasts in grammar

We have constantly been making the point that changes in the tonality in an utterance signal changes in the organization of information as perceived by the speaker. We have thus been highlighting the role of tonality in the informational function of intonation. Even the cases of marked tonality relate to the way the speaker is managing the organization of information, by having a theme different to the subject of the clause and by adding adjuncts that comment on the information or relate to the addressee.

But we have also seen that intonation in English fulfils a grammatical function too. First of all, intonation units often match clauses, even to the extent that the boundaries of intonation units and clauses coincide. Look at this example and think out the way you may say it:

(2.38)   When you enter the waiting room is on the left

Did you need two tries? Most people do. Most people read it first as if *the waiting room* is the direct object complementing the verb *enter*, and then realize that that cannot be right because then there is no subject for the verb *is*.

On a second try, you prepare yourself to treat *the waiting room* as the 'missing' subject of *is*, and that leaves you with *enter* as an intransitive verb and as the end of the first clause. On this second try you would say *when you enter* as one intonation unit with a boundary before *the waiting room*, and thus the boundary between the two units coincides with the boundary between the two clauses. (We concede, as we did in Chapter 1, that a comma after *enter* would make the clause boundary clear; but we point out, as also we did in Chapter 1, that commas belong to the written mode, but that it is intonation that performs such a function in the spoken form, and secondly, that writers are notoriously inconsistent in their use of commas in any case.)

The second way in which the role of intonation is seen in English grammar is in disambiguating parallel wordings that contrast in syntactic structure. We discussed two examples in Chapter 1 that involve contrasts in tonality: (1.8) and (1.9), and (1.20) and (1.21).

7.1   Defining and non-defining items

Remind yourself of the difference between (1.8) and (1.9):

(1.8)   My brother who lives in Nai<u>ro</u>bi |...

(1.9)   My <u>bro</u>ther | who lives in Nai<u>ro</u>bi |...

In (1.8), the relative clause defines which brother is meant, i.e. not the one who lives anywhere else; it restricts the reference. The relative clause in (1.9) does **not** define which brother is meant; it adds extra information; it does not restrict the reference, and you might justifiably assume that there is in fact only one brother to refer to; as we have previously noted, such non-defining clauses could well be labelled 'adding clauses'. In spoken discourse, it is the tonality – part of the intonation system – that differentiates between the identical wording of the two cases. (Remember: any comma belongs to writing.)

The distinction between defining and non-defining extends to phrases, too. Compare

(2.39)   The man dressed in <u>black</u> | (then stood up)

(2.39a)   The man | dressed in <u>black</u> | (then stood up)

and again

(2.40)   The man in <u>black</u> | (then stood up)

(2.40a)   The <u>man</u> | in <u>black</u> | (then stood up)

The tonality break after *man* in (2.39a) and (2.40a) indicates that the following clause or phrase does not define *the man*, but adds extra information – which might be incidental or highly relevant.

Now compare

(2.41)   The man with the dog sitting near the <u>bus</u> stop | (is in trouble)

(2.42)   The man with the <u>dog</u> | sitting near the <u>bus</u> stop | (is in trouble)

The second, (2.42), seems to suggest that it is the man who is sitting near the bus stop, as additional, non-defining information; but the first, (2.41), strongly suggests that it is the dog that is doing the sitting, because the sitting defines which dog is meant!

See how many meanings you can work out in the next example:

(2.43)   The man and the woman dressed in black (then stood up)

If you have no intonation unit boundaries until *then*, then you are defining the man and the woman by distinguishing them from other men and women who are not dressed in black. If you have a boundary after *man*, then the defining clause is limited to *the woman*; in other words there must be more than one woman in the situation, but not necessarily more than one man. And if you have a boundary only after *woman*, then the following clause *dressed in black* will be interpreted as an additional, but not a defining, piece of information. Compare them for yourself:

(2.43a)   The man and the woman dressed in <u>black</u> | (then stood up)

(2.43b)   The <u>man</u> | and the woman dressed in <u>black</u> | (then stood up)

(2.43c)   The man and the <u>wo</u>man | dressed in <u>black</u> | (then stood up)

It may appear complicated at first, but it is in fact a straightforward matter of intonation performing a grammatical function consistently and affecting the meaning consistently too.

7.2   Apposition

Apposition is the relationship between two or more items which are either identical in reference or else the reference of one must be included in the reference of the other. In

(2.44)   Tom Jones, the singer, comes from South Wales

there is identity of reference between the two appositional items *Tom Jones* and *the singer*. In

(2.45)   The Government, the prime minister and his cabinet, are pushing
          for a quick decision

the prime minister and his cabinet is included within the notion of *The
Government.*

There are two ways of saying the first example, and the difference is
parallel to that between defining and non-defining items. You can say it as

(2.44a)   Tom <u>Jones</u> | the <u>singer</u> | comes from South <u>Wales</u>

in which case *the singer* is added as extra information. However, in

(2.44b)   Tom Jones the <u>singer</u> | comes from South <u>Wales</u>

the singer does identify which Tom Jones is meant, since in South Wales
there are hundreds of Tom Joneses; the Tom Jones of Fielding's novel is not
meant either.

The distinction between defining and non-defining apposition is thus
indicated solely by intonation in the spoken mode, and consistently at that. (In
the written mode we note, again, an inconsistency in the use of commas.)
However, it might also be noted that non-defining apposition can be
introduced by a formula such as *that is, that is to say, in other words*, etc., as in

(2.44c)   Tom <u>Jones</u> | that is the <u>singer</u> | comes from South <u>Wales</u>

Such formulas do not affect the intonation; the tonality remains the same for
non-defining items and the formula is incorporated into the intonation unit
accompanying the second item.

Quirk et al. (1972: 626–7) cite three cases of potential ambiguity between
instances of apposition and the more complicated types of
complementation. In speech, disambiguation is effected through intonation.
The first example is this:

(2.46a)   They sent Joan a waitress from the ho<u>tel</u>

As a single intonation unit, this would be interpreted as *a waitress from the
hotel* being sent to Joan, i.e. as a double transitive clause, *Joan* as indirect
object, *a waitress from the hotel* as direct object. But can you think of other
ways of saying that clause? What if you put an intonation unit boundary after
Joan?

(2.46b)   They sent <u>Joan</u> | a waitress from the ho<u>tel</u>

Now, in this rendering, *Joan* is the waitress from the hotel. But what if you
add a second boundary after *waitress?*

(2.46c)   They sent <u>Joan</u> | a <u>wait</u>ress | from the ho<u>tel</u>

In this rendering, *Joan* is still a waitress, but now she is sent away from the
hotel. Tonality is doing both grammatical and informational work in this
case, but it should make clear how intonation is sometimes absolutely crucial

in conveying a concise message.

Here is Quirk et al.'s second example:

(2.47a)   They considered Miss Hartley a very good <u>teac</u>her

As a single intonation unit, this would be interpreted as a clause with a direct object complementing *considered,* and a further object complement to *Miss Hartley,* meaning: 'Miss Hartley was considered a very good teacher.' But in

(2.47b)   They considered Miss <u>Har</u>tley | a very good <u>teac</u>her

you have a case of non-defining apposition – an extra piece of information is added.

Their third example is

(2.48a)   They called Susan a <u>wait</u>ress

As a single unit, this is parallel to (2.46a), so that *Susan* is an indirect object, and *a waitress* is a direct object, both complementing *called.* But in

(2.48b)   They called <u>Su</u>san | a <u>wait</u>ress

a waitress is, once again, a non-defining appositional item.

Apposition may take the form of clauses as well as noun phrases, and in many cases clauses in apposition become relative clauses. Here are some examples from Quirk et al. (1972: 645–8):

(2.49)   They put it where it was <u>light</u> | where everybody could <u>see</u> it

(2.50)   He told them the <u>news</u> | that the troops would be <u>lea</u>ving

(2.51)   Their sol<u>u</u>tion | to appoint a com<u>mi</u>ttee | is dep<u>lo</u>rable

(2.52)   For them to pay him a com<u>mi</u>ssion | <u>his</u> suggestion | seemed an excellent i<u>dea</u>

These are all cases of non-defining apposition. An instance of defining apposition corresponding to (2.50) might be

(2.53)   The news that the troops would be <u>lea</u>ving | has been an<u>nou</u>nced

The clause *that the troops would be leaving* defined which news was to be announced, but in (2.54) it does not:

(2.54)   The <u>news</u> | that the troops would be <u>lea</u>ving | has been an<u>nou</u>nced

Apposition may also take the form of other clause elements; for example:
(i) predicates (see Quirk et al., 1972: 645–8):

(2.55)   They summoned <u>help</u> | called the police and <u>fire</u> brigade

(ii) complements:

(2.56)   She is <u>be</u>tter | <u>ve</u>ry much better

(iii) adjuncts:

(2.57)   <u>Third</u>ly | and <u>last</u>ly | they would not accept his <u>pro</u>mise

(2.58)   They bought it <u>cheap</u>ly | for three <u>do</u>llars

Finally, a few other cases where differences in tonality affect the interpretation of syntactic structure:

(2.59a)   John looked a <u>cu</u>rious man (subjective complement)

(2.59b)   John <u>looked</u> | a <u>cu</u>rious man (apposition, implying 'because he was ...')

Similarly

(2.60a)   He <u>died</u> a <u>hap</u>py <u>man</u> (subjective complement)

(2.60b)   He <u>died</u> | a happy <u>man</u> (apposition, implying 'he'd always been a happy man')

Also

(2.61a)   I rested con<u>tent</u> (subjective complement)

(2.61b)   I <u>rested</u> | con<u>tent</u> (apposition, implying 'because I was content ...')

(2.62a)   Bill left very <u>angry</u> (subjective complement)

(2.62b)   Bill <u>left</u> | very <u>angry</u> (apposition, implying 'because Bill was very angry...')

and finally

(2.63a)   That's a<u>no</u>ther thing I don't know yet (rankshifted clause, post-modifying *thing*)

(2.63b)   That's a<u>no</u>ther thing | I don't <u>know</u> yet (apposition)

7.3   Verb phrases

A verb phrase can be simple: with a single lexical verb; or complex: with more than one lexical verb, e.g. *(You must) try to stop smoking.* Some instances of complex verbal phrases look very similar to a series of verbs, for instance, compare

(2.64)   He began <u>smo</u>king

(2.65)   He began to <u>smoke</u>

(2.66)   He stopped <u>smo</u>king

(2.67)   He <u>stopped</u> | to <u>smoke</u>

The pair (2.66) and (2.67) may look at first as if they are parallel to the pair (2.64) and (2.65). (2.64) and (2.65) have different structures but share, broadly, the same meaning. (2.66) is the real opposite to (2.64) and (2.65), but shares the structure of only (2.64). (2.67) may look superficially the parallel to (2.65), but it does in fact have a different structure, and quite a different meaning. The verb phrases in (2.64), (2.65) and (2.66) are all complex, but they are each a single phrase in a single clause. In (2.67), we have two simple verb phrases: the first belongs to a main clause, and the second to the following 'purpose' clause, which could be reworded as *in order to smoke*, which helps to make it clearer. Because (2.67) consists of two clauses, the normal, neutral, tonality is expected: two clauses and two intonation units.

However, there are a few cases where a complex verbal phrase has an identical wording with a series of verbs in separate clauses. Here is an example:

(2.68a)   He came to <u>hear</u> about it

(2.68b)   He <u>came</u> | to <u>hear</u> about it

(2.68a) involves a complex verbal phrase as an idiom meaning 'it happened by chance that ...', but because it constitutes only one verbal phrase, it is the predicate of only one clause; hence only one intonation unit. (2.68b), on the other hand, has a main clause followed by a 'purpose' clause (rather like (2.67)), i.e. two clauses; hence, two intonation units.

Here is another example:

(2.69a)   He left me to get on with the <u>job</u>

(2.69b)   He <u>left</u> me | to get on with the <u>job</u>

(2.69a) has a single, though complex, verbal phrase: one clause, one intonation unit; (2.69b) is a series of two clauses. You might notice an extra, subtle difference in meaning in this pair; who, in each case, gets on with the job?!

Other pairs of examples are:

(2.70a)   Bill helped to avoid an <u>accident</u>

(2.70b)   Bill <u>helped</u> | to avoid an <u>accident</u>

(2.71a)   Bill looked to be on the <u>safe</u> side

(2.71b)   Bill <u>looked</u> | to be on the <u>safe</u> side

7.4   Negative domain

Another well-known case of parallel wording of two different syntactic structures offers entirely opposite meanings. If a main clause has a negative and is followed by *because* and a reason, or by *so (that)* and a result, then intonation – in the shape of tonality – performs the crucial role of differentiating the syntactic structures and meanings. Look at the following statement and try and work out two meanings for it which are entirely opposite to each other:

(2.72)   I didn't come because he told me

How many clauses are there? Two: *I didn't come* and *because* ... If you consider the case of neutral tonality first, i.e. two intonational units, each 'covering' one clause, then the meaning is quite clear: the person did not come, and a reason for not coming is added:

(2.72a)   I didn't <u>come</u> | because he <u>told</u> me

If, however, you run the two clauses together into a single intonation unit, you get quite a different meaning: the person did go, but not for the reason that is given - he/she went for some other reason:

(2.72b)   I didn't come because he <u>told</u> me

(This would normally be spoken with a fall-rise on *told me*, and implies: 'I came for some other reason.')

   It seems to be the case that the domain of the negative extends to the next tonality boundary; thus in (2.72a), it is *come* that is negativized, but in (2.72b), it is *because he told me* that is negativized. ((2.72b) could be rendered as *It is not because he told me that I came*, implying: 'I came for some other reason'; but note that this is not the most obvious way to give such a message; (2.72b) is, in fact, the most obvious way, with reliance upon the effect of intonation.)

   Now consider a *so that* clause:

(2.73)   He didn't go so that he could get promotion

Like the preceding example, this sentence has a structure of two clauses, and on that basis we would expect two intonation units:

(2.73a)   He didn't <u>go</u> | so that he could get pro<u>mo</u>tion

This suggests a meaning in which the person decided to stay in order to get promotion. The domain of the negative extends to the next tonality boundary and thus *go* is negativized. But in the marked tonality case - one intonation unit covering the two clauses - it is the *so that* clause that is negativized:

(2.73b)   He didn't go so that he could get pro<u>mo</u>tion

This rendering implies that the person did go, but not in order to get promotion, but to gain some other result.

   In both cases of marked tonality, (2.72b) and (2.73b), the negative is transferred to the following clause; and marked tonality - a contrast in intonation - is the typical way in which English speakers achieve this.

7.5   Report clauses

Report clauses are those that take the following form:

(2.74)   He said he would <u>come</u>

(2.75)   I reported that they had taken a de<u>ci</u>sion

(2.76)   They asked if he knew the de<u>ci</u>sion

(2.77)   He didn't know whether they had already de<u>ci</u>ded

(2.78)   We very much hope they will <u>think</u> about it

There is an initial verb of 'reporting' (which has to be interpreted rather broadly to include asking, knowing, hoping, etc.) and a clause containing the content of what is 'reported'. The two parts are usually linked by a conjunction, e.g. *that, whether, if,* but the *that* conjunction may be omitted. It is best to regard the two parts as a single clause consisting of the main verb of 'reporting' and a (rankshifted) clause as the direct object complementing the 'reporting' verb. Not all linguists describe report clauses in this way,[6] but it seems best to, since in all the above cases a single intonation unit 'covers' the whole statement. Read them for yourself. (Notice also that one single intonation unit is still sufficient even if the 'reporting' verb is placed at the end, e.g. *He would come, he said; They had taken a decision, I reported,* and also if the statements were converted into interrogatives or imperatives, e.g. *Did he say he would come? Ask if he knew the decision.*)

The difference between report clauses and direct speech is matched by intonation. The direct speech version of (2.74) might have been *He said, 'I will come',* which would be rendered in speech as two intonation units:

(2.79)   He <u>said</u> | I'll <u>come</u>

with a little pause after *said.* Notice that the wording of reporting and direct speech might occasionally be identical:

(2.80a)   And then he'll say who's <u>com</u>ing (reporting)

(2.80b)   And then he'll <u>say</u> | who's <u>com</u>ing (direct: *And then he will say, 'Who is coming?'*)

Compare reporting and direct speech in this pair:

(2.81)   Tell me where your <u>bro</u>ther is (reporting)

(2.82)   <u>Tell</u> me | where is your <u>bro</u>ther (direct: *Tell me, 'Where is your brother?'*)

The wording is almost the same, but again the intonation is quite different.

Now see if you can work out the difference in meaning between this pair of examples with identical wording:

(2.83)   Tell him to save <u>time</u>

(2.84)   <u>Tell</u> him | to save <u>time</u>

(2.83) follows the normal pattern for report clauses and means the equivalent of 'Tell him to hurry up'. (2.84) seems to imply 'Don't let him work it out for himself because that will waste time; by telling him, time will be saved', i.e. main clause followed by a dependent 'purpose' clause (*in order to*).

Report clause structures with *know* need to be distinguished from linking adjuncts, particularly *you know*.

(2.85a)   You know it's im<u>por</u>tant

is a report clause (*it's important* is the direct object complementing the verb *know*), but in

(2.85b)   You know | it's important

the *you know* is acting as a means of linking a previous utterance with the new one in the following, main, clause.

7.6   Clause complements

Verbs vary in the kind of complementation they require in the rest of the clause. Verbs may be intransitive and require no further complementation; other verbs are transitive, some requiring a direct object as complement, others requiring an additional, indirect, object complement as well.[7] Some verbs may sometimes operate as intransitive and sometimes as transitive, e.g. *enter*, as we saw above (p.40). Another example is *wash*, and we have already seen how intonation helps in distinguishing *wash* (transitive) from *wash* (intransitive). Remind yourself of the difference between (1.20) and (1.21):

(1.20)   She washed and brushed her <u>hair</u>

(1.21)   She <u>washed</u> | and brushed her <u>hair</u>

In (1.20) she washed her hair (as well as brushed it); *her hair* is the direct object complementing the verb *wash*, which is thus transitive. In (1.21), however, *washed* is intransitive, since the boundary separates that verb from the following words. We also saw in the previous discussion that other verbs which may sometimes be transitive and sometimes intransitive will also need intonation to disambiguate between parallel wordings. This, as we saw then, is intonation doing grammatical work.

There is another situation where intonation is necessary to disambiguate parallel wordings that involve complements. In colloquial speech, the real subject of a clause is sometimes left to the end, for effect, e.g. *They're good, aren't they, these arrows* (referring to the illuminated arrows at dangerous bends in the road, that show up in the dark). This displacement of the subject is much more common than most people realize, in informal speech, and can lead, possibly, to confusion if the displaced subject occurs after verbs which can either be transitive or intransitive. Halliday (1967: 42) gives the following example:

(2.86a)   They've <u>left</u> | the <u>o</u>thers

in which *the others* is the 'real', but displaced, subject, with the meaning, 'The others have left (actually)'. *To leave* is a verb that can either be intransitive as it is in (2.86a), or transitive as in (2.86b):

(2.86b)   They've left the others

In this case, *the others* is the direct object complementing *left*. (We concede again the point that this difference might be shown clearly in the written form by using a comma appropriately; but in the spoken form, it is intonation that does the grammatical work.)

Here is another pair of examples:

(2.87a)   She's helping | Ann

(2.87b)   She's helping Ann

You should be able easily to work out in which case Ann is helping or being helped.

8. Intonation unit boundaries

One final, but obvious, question to ask is how we know where the boundaries lie. In many circumstances there is no problem: if an utterance consists of a single intonation unit, then it is bounded by silence before and after. If an utterance consists of two or more units of intonation with clear pauses which exactly coincide with sentence or clause boundaries, then again there is no problem.

But problems do arise, and especially so in fast informal speech. Here is an example from Brown, Currie and Kenworthy (1980: 42):

(2.88)

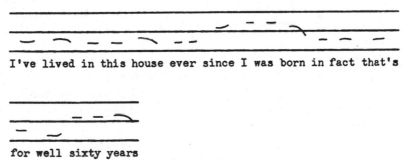

I've lived in this house ever since I was born in fact that's

for well sixty years

The problem, they explain, arises with the phrase *in fact*. You can see that its pitch is relatively low and comes after a fall; it also comes before a new clause. (There is no point, of course, in appealing to commas, since this text was spoken before it received any written form.) The pitch movements on *house, born* and *years* suggest at least three intonation units; but what about *in fact?* It could either belong to the unit that contains *ever since I was born*, or it could be part of the following unit, which would make it *in fact that's for well sixty years*, or, thirdly, it could be a short intonation unit of its own.

Although many examples of this kind of problem arise in the course of analysis of informal spoken text, there are principles with which we operate so that most of the time we can identify the boundaries. Crystal (1969: 204-7) has the fullest account of the phonetic cues we use in the identification of intonation unit boundaries. He claims that there are certain regular patterns of features, but two principal ones. Firstly, there is a perceivable pitch change at some point following a tonic syllable: either a stepping up after a falling tone, or a stepping down after a rise; if the pitch of the tonic syllable was level, then either a stepping up or down would signal the start of a new intonation unit. Secondly, there is either a (very) slight pause or a change of pace in the flow of syllables; syllables at the end of a unit tend to be relatively slower, but syllables at the beginning of a unit have a tendency to speed up. Very often, all three features appear: a change of pitch, a pause and a change of pace, but equally often only one feature will be employed.

The identification of the boundaries is not necessarily a crucial issue. Pike (1945) maintained that phonological units usually do have 'fuzzy edges'; how do you identify, for instance, the boundaries of consonants and vowels, especially in the light of instrumental evidence of continual overlap? Other linguists have maintained that it is not absolutely necessary to identify boundaries precisely.[8] Indeed, there is often a smooth transition from one unit to another without a pause, and Halliday, for one, has incorporated this feature into his description by talking of compound tones: a fall followed by a rise is the most typical case.

Where there are cases of dispute, where Crystal's phonetic criteria do not produce a clear-cut boundary, then we have no option but to appeal to grammatical or semantic criteria. This is because the vast majority of cases do coincide with some kind of grammatical boundary (not just between clauses, but between clause elements, instances of apposition, words in lists, etc.) and do coincide with the organization of information into 'pieces'. The principle here is that you interpret difficult data by principles established in easier data, but even then, some problems like Brown, Currie and Kenworthy's *in fact* remain unresolved.

Unresolved cases in the analysis of tonality should not undermine the general theory that has been presented in this chapter. Such cases are relatively infrequent, as a perusal of the transcription of intonation in informal speech would testify. The general theory is that when people communicate in speech, they must organize and manage their information into discrete pieces of information which are then worded and formulated grammatically and pronounced in intonation units. The theory also specifies that a speaker's perception of their organization of information is presented in a single unit of intonation, which is typically contained within a single clause. Where there is this congruence of semantic, phonological and grammatical units, tonality is said to be neutral; where there is not, tonality is said to be marked, and this chapter has presented a comprehensive coverage of marked tonality. There is always a congruence of units of information and units of intonation.[9]

It must also be conceded that units of information do not always seem to contain much in the way of information. Units often only contain exclamations like *Coo!*, *My goodness me!*, or displays of colloquial style like *you know*, *I mean*, *you see* or of back channel like *mm*, *yes*. Sometimes they only contain 'running repairs' when the speaker realizes that something they have said does not correspond to standard grammar or that a better word could have been chosen. The term 'unit of information' has therefore to be defined relatively broadly: it is the semantico-phonological unit for the development of discourse, which handles not only information as propositional content but also markers of style, expressions of attitudes and feelings, 'running repairs', 'phatic communion' like *Good morning* and *How do you do?* and politeness formulas like *please, thank you* and *don't mention it.*

See if you can work out a reasonable tonality analysis of the opening two paragraphs of *Treasure Island*, imagining that you have to read it out to an audience.

Squire Trelawney, Dr. Livesey, and the rest of these gentlemen having asked me to write down the whole particulars about Treasure Island, from the beginning to the end, keeping nothing back but the bearings of the island, and that only because there is still treasure not yet lifted, I take up my pen in the year of grace 17–, and go back to the time when my father kept the 'Admiral Benbow' inn, and the brown old seaman, with the sabre cut, first took up his lodging under our roof.

I remember him as if it were yesterday, as he came plodding to the inn door, his sea-chest following behind him in a hand-barrow; a tall, strong, heavy, nut-brown man; his tarry pigtail falling over the shoulders of his soiled blue coat; his hands ragged and scarred, with black, broken nails; and the sabre cut across one cheek, a dirty, livid white. I remember him looking round the cove and whistling to himself as he did so, and then breaking out in that old sea-song that he sang so often after-wards:–

'Fifteen men on the Dead Man's Chest –
Yo-ho-ho, and a bottle of rum!'

in the high, old tottering voice that seemed to have been tuned and broken at the capstan bars.

Now try the next text, from *Pygmalion*, which is designed to be read aloud, but from which the punctuation helps have been removed.

HIGGINS. There Thats all youll get out of Eliza Ah-ah-ow-oo! No use explaining As a military man you ought to know that Give her her orders: thats enough for her Eliza you are to live here for the next six months learning how to speak beautifully like a lady in a florist's shop If you are good and do whatever youre told you shall sleep in a proper bedroom and have lots to eat and money to buy chocolates and take rides in taxis If youre naughty and idle you will sleep in the back kitchen among the black beetles and be walloped by Mrs Pearce with a broomstick At the end of six months you shall go to Buckingham Palace in a carriage beautifully dressed If the King finds out youre not a lady you will be taken by the police to the Tower of London where your head will be cut off as a warning to other presumptuous flower girls If you are not found out you shall have a present of seven-and-sixpence to start life as a lady in a shop if you refuse this offer you will be a most ungrateful wicked girl and the angels will weep for you [*To Pickering*] Now are you satisfied Pickering [*To Mrs Pearce*] Can I put it more plainly and fairly Mrs Pearce

(Penguin edn: 45–6)

Notes

1. 'Tone group' is Halliday's term for **intonation unit**; others refer to it as 'tone unit', 'intonation group', 'breath group', 'phonological phrase', 'phonological clause', and 'intonational phrase'!

2. See Quirk et al. (1964); Tench (1990: 41–53).

3. Halliday (1967: 17, 42–3) argued the case for a special 'listing' pre-tonic, but this is refuted in Tench (1990: 350–4). See also Crystal (1975: 19) on 'structural parallelism'.

4. For a full exposition of theme and rheme, see Halliday (1985: chapters 3 and 8).

5. It has to be noted that this is not a view shared by all grammarians. A fuller discussion will be found in Tench (1990: 110–16).

6. Sinclair (1972) and Young (1980) describe such structures as two consecutive independent clauses, but the intonational evidence is one reason for rejecting such a view.

7. For a full description of clause complementation, see e.g. Young (1980).

8. See Halliday (1967: 19 footnote), Gibbon (1976: 66), Brazil, Coulthard and Johns (1980: 45–6). Brown, Currie and Kenworthy (1980) abandoned the attempt to achieve principles of analysis in the identification of intonation unit boundaries, but see Tench (1990: 170–83).

9. This is why Halliday's notion of 'compound tones' with 'one and a half pieces of information' is not promoted here; it blurs the main principle. See Tench (1990: 166–70).

3

Tonicity

THE FOCAL POINT OF INTONATION

1. Tonic syllables

In the previous chapter we looked at the function and the nature of the units of intonation: in this chapter we look at the heart of these units, the tonic syllable, which is the indispensable minimum. We have had reason to note how some intonation units are abandoned as a speaker restarts what they want to say; we describe units as being abandoned precisely on this point: they lack a tonic syllable. If the speaker does not reach the tonic syllable in any given intonation unit, then we do not have enough clues to decide on the structure and the focus of information in that particular part of the message. We will therefore begin this chapter with a consideration of the answers to two obvious questions: what is a tonic syllable? and, what does it do?

It is usually affirmed that the tonic syllable is the most prominent, or salient, of the stressed syllables in any given intonation unit. This traditional statement has been challenged in the light of actual difficulties in attempts to identify tonic syllables in recordings of natural, spontaneous, informal speech. The challenge itself has been met with more vigorous experimentation which has resulted in a much clearer understanding of the nature of phonetic prominence in intonation units.[1]

Seven features appear to be significant for the identification of tonic syllables:

1. pitch peak (i.e. maximum pitch height)
2. maximum pitch range
3. kinetic tone
4. loudness peak (i.e. maximum intensity)
5. decrescendo
6. tempo marking
7. pause

'Pitch peak' clearly refers to the highest pitched syllable within a given intonation unit; by 'maximum pitch range' we recognize that a number of syllables will exhibit pitch movement, but that one will exhibit greater movement, than others. Kinetic tone also involves pitch movement; in this case, we recognize that usually there is one syllable with a degree of movement, even if all the others are fairly stable at a fixed pitch level.[2] These three features constitute the role played by pitch.

'Loudness peak' clearly refers to the loudest syllable within a given intonation unit. By 'decrescendo', we refer to an observable decrease in perceived loudness in the succession of syllables following a tonic syllable; in other words, syllables following a tonic syllable are often less loud than the syllables preceding the tonic, in the pre-tonic segment. These two features constitute the role played by loudness.

'Tempo marking' refers to the relative speed of delivery in the syllable concerned; the tonic syllable is marked by an absence of quickening, i.e. it remains as relatively long compared to surrounding syllables. Occasionally, the syllable before a tonic is so long that it can be described as a 'drawl'. Furthermore, the identification of a tonic syllable may be aided by a slight pause preceding it. These two features constitute the role played by timing, although it must be conceded that the role of timing is much less pronounced than either pitch or loudness. However, it can be seen that the three traditionally labelled 'prosodic features' – pitch, volume and duration – together provide the basis of the way in which speakers produce tonic syllables and learners identify them.

It is also maintained that different combinations of these features produced different reactions. If six, or all seven, features combine, maximal prominence is produced which learners interpret as strongly contrastive. In other words, if a speaker wishes to be seen as contrasting one part of their message with something already said or implied, the tendency would be to 'fire on all cylinders' and use all features.

However, speakers are not always contrasting parts of their messages with other items in the discourse, and are, consequently, content to use less than all seven features, indeed to use only four features to project the tonic syllable. The four features are kinetic tone, decrescendo, either pitch peak or maximum pitch range, and, fourthly, either loudness peak, tempo marking or pause. This is the phonetic basis of tonicity; in cases of uncertainty, the analyst must consult semantic or syntactic criteria, as in the matter of dubious intonation unit boundaries. However, in the vast majority of cases, it is possible not only to identify a tonic syllable, but also to secure general agreement among a group of listeners.[3]

Figure 3.1 is an instrumental reading which shows the pitch, the volume and the relative length of the tonic syllable. The top two graphs indicate loudness, the bottom graph pitch, and time is indicated linearly.

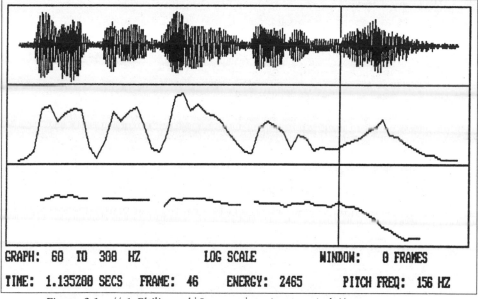

```
GRAPH:  60  TO  300  HZ          LOG SCALE          WINDOW:     0 FRAMES
TIME:  1.135200 SECS   FRAME:  46   ENERGY:  2465      PITCH FREQ:  156 HZ
```

Figure 3.1   // .1. Philip and | Jean are | getting <u>married</u> //

The tonic syllable, then, is that syllable in a given intonation unit which is made most prominent by a combination of pitch, volume and length. But what is its function? Why is it there? Halliday (1970: 40) explains: 'The function of the tonic is to form the focus of information: to express what the speaker decides to make the main point or burden of the message.' This is a vital contribution that Halliday has made to our understanding of the function of intonation in any language. As we have already seen, the units of intonation represent the speaker's management of the organization of information: one unit of intonation represents one unit of information. Now we can add to the theory, and say that the tonic represents the focus of each unit of information.

We can illustrate the function of the tonic quite easily from an example of contrasting tonicity which was often used to help new learners of English.[4] The following question can be asked in quite a number of different ways by altering the tonic syllable; the most obvious way is to have the tonic syllable as the last word:

(3.1a)   Can you break an apple in <u>two</u>?

The intonation starts off quite high on the word *Can*, gradually descends through *you break an apple in*, and then rises on *two*. *Two* is the tonic and is made prominent by the combination of prosodic features referred to above.

But what difference is made if you shift the tonic to *apple*?

(3.1b)   Can you break an <u>ap</u>ple in two?

55

The focus of attention switches to *apple*. (3.1b) could really only make sense if people had already been talking about breaking things in two, and the new focus of information is on a new item being offered for consideration.

Notice that by changing the tonic, you change the focus of information. Try the same sentence with *break* as tonic:

(3.1c)   Can you <u>break</u> an apple in two?

Wouldn't this suggest that the focus of information is now on *breaking*, probably in contrast to some other action like cutting?

And wouldn't the next rendering suggest that *you* becomes the focus of information, probably in contrast to somebody else?

(3.1d)   Can <u>you</u> break an apple in two?

And, finally, a fifth possibility would involve the tonic on *Can*:

(3.1e)   <u>Can</u> you break an apple in two?

The focus of information is now on the ability of the person addressed. Perhaps he or she has indicated the idea that breaking an apple in two presents no problem; but then comes a query, or even a direct challenge, in the form of (3.1e).

As the tonic is changed, so is the focus of information. In each rendering of (3.1), we are presented with only one unit of intonation, but with five different focuses. In more technical terms, we can say that whereas the tonality has remained constant, the tonicity has been changed each time.

2. Neutral tonicity

As with tonality, there is a neutral form in the tonicity system. The system of tonicity is the range of choices in the position that the tonic syllable can have in a given intonation unit. This was illustrated earlier, in Chapter 1, in the discussion of the different possible renderings of

(1.5)   What are you going to do tonight?

and has now been illustrated again with variations (3.1a) to (3.1e).

The neutral form of the tonicity system is to have the tonic syllable within the last lexical item in the intonation unit. We described (3.1a) as being 'the most obvious way' to intone that question, and you will notice that the tonic syllable is in the last lexical item, *two*. If you would care to check through Chapters 1 and 2, you will see that since we started marking the tonic syllable from item (1.10) onwards, the vast majority of the examples have the tonic syllable within the last lexical item. Look through and check for yourself. Crystal (1975: 23) stated that, in his data, the tonic accompanied the last lexical item 80 per cent of the time. In newsreading, the proportion reaches as high as 88 per cent (Tench, 1990: 497), but it is noticeable that whatever the 'genre' of spoken discourse might be, this generally high proportion is always retained.[5]

Halliday maintained that this propensity of the tonic to accompany the last lexical item has significance for the structure of information within the clause, and that this end position is the normal position unless there is good reason for it to be otherwise. Notice that we have been careful to specify that the item concerned must be a lexical item – not a grammatical item, not even the last word. The lexical item has semantic significance and may often contain more than a single word: compounds, e.g. *station master, railway track, signal failure*, etc., or phrasal verbs, e.g. *to take off, to get in, to come across*, etc., or idioms. Grammatical items are usually described as having structural significance, like pronouns, articles, prepositions, auxiliary verbs, etc., but Halliday includes all items that belong to closed systems, like *here/there, now/then, yesterday/today/tonight, together, again*, etc. That is why the most obvious way of saying (1.5) is to put the tonic not on the last word *tonight*, but on the last truly lexical item, *do*.

The most obvious way of saying (3.1) was to place the tonic on *two*, as if the context was as vague as 'What are you going to ask now?' The context for (3.1b), however, has to be much more specific: 'I can see that you can break things in two – so ...' Similarly, the contexts for all the other renderings would be specific, although different in each case. The context provides the kind of information that is 'given', and the tonic conveys what the speaker considers to be 'new'. Look again at (3.1b) to (3.1e) and see what is given and what is new information. The tonic syllable indicates what is new.

Halliday pointed out that the normal structure of given and new information in a clause is to present the given first and the new last, and that is why the tonic syllable usually comes at the end. But the context of (3.1a) is so vague that the **whole** of the clause could be regarded as new, and so we now need to introduce the distinction between **broad focus** and **narrow focus**.

3. Broad focus

Imagine two or more people together and one of them suddenly makes a decision and says:

(3.2)   I think I'll go and have a cup of tea

The natural place for the tonic will be *tea*, as the last lexical item. None of the information is given, in the sense that you can recover it from the context (except, possibly, *I*). The whole sentence contains only new information, but the tonic syllable cannot occur with each lexical item – otherwise you would have several messages, instead of just one. The speaker says (3.2) as a single piece of information. The tonic indicates the **end** of the new information; it is not as if the speaker is merely focusing on *tea*; he or she is focusing on the whole plan of going and having a cup of tea. The focus is broad; it embraces the whole clause.

Here is another example. Imagine two people together, and perhaps there comes a lull in the conversation which is broken by a general question like:

(3.3)   Where are you going on your holidays?

The natural place for the tonic is again the last lexical item, *holidays*. None of the information is given (except, perhaps, *you*) because this utterance is the opening of a new topic. The question contains only new information; the focus is, therefore, not confined just to *holidays*, but it embraces *where* and *going*, too. The focus is broad, embracing the whole clause.

A third example takes the form of a *yes/no* question:

(3.4)   Did you have a nice time?

Again, this may be an opening, perhaps, of a new subtopic within the general topic of holidays. The whole clause has broad focus.

Finally, an example with an imperative:

(3.5)   Look at that man up there

This again has broad focus if it is said as an opening to a new topic of conversation. Like the others, (3.2)-(3.4), the tonic falls on the last lexical item. (*There* belongs to a closed system and *up* is a preposition, and so they do not count as lexical items.)

Broad focus has been illustrated above in four different clause types to emphasize the point that information structure is not confined by grammatical structure. It has also been illustrated as openings, but it is just as relevant in the progress of a narrative. Here is an example of part of a narrative from Crystal and Davy (1975: 44); each intonation unit is reproduced on a separate line:

(3.6) (Yes I remember there was a terrible story – horrifying story that was told by a
        colleague of mine when I used to teach years ago – who erm ...)

This chap lived in erm – a semi detached <u>house</u>
and next <u>door</u>
– there was a <u>man</u>
who'd just bought a new <u>car</u>
– and he was <u>tel</u>ling me
that one <u>mor</u>ning
he was looking through the <u>win</u>dow
– and this . <u>man</u>
allowed his <u>wife</u> to drive the car
very un<u>wise</u>ly
and she was having a first <u>go</u> in it
– and – he <u>backed</u> it

<u>out</u> of the garage
– so that it was standing on the <u>drive</u>way
, and he'd closed the garage doors
– and she came out of the <u>house</u>
– to take this <u>car</u> out
very <u>gin</u>gerly
– and opened the <u>door</u>
– and sat in the <u>car</u>
– and – er . began to <u>back</u>
very very <u>gent</u>ly
taking . <u>great</u> care you see
that she didn't do <u>any</u>thing to this . to this new car
– and – – as she <u>backed</u>
– there was an unpleasant . <u>crunch</u>ing sound
and she <u>slapped</u> on the brakes
and looked around <u>frant</u>ically
– and realized
that she hadn't opened the . <u>gates</u>
. that . let on to the main <u>road</u> you see

Now read through the extract again and see how frequently the tonic coincides with the last lexical item of each unit; notice, too, how often in these cases of neutral tonicity the focus of information is broad, containing exclusively new information – not always, but pretty often.

Broad focus, then, refers to instances of intonation units containing only new information. However, there is the odd case of the reverse being true too, where intonation units contain only given information. Heard at a conference was the following remark:

(3.7)   I'd love to attend the <u>next</u> one

meaning the next conference; *one* is functioning as a pronoun here and so *next* is the final lexical item. The rejoinder to (3.7) came as follows:

(3.8)   You'd love to attend the <u>next</u> one!?

said with some surprise, but with identical wording apart from the obvious necessary substitution of pronouns. There is no new information as such in (3.8); it is all given. In such cases, the focus in the rejoinder has to be treated as parallel to that of the original. If (3.7) has broad focus, (3.8) must be treated as having broad focus, too.

4. Narrow focus

Imagine, again, the situation in which one person decides suddenly to go and have a cup of tea (3.2); if someone then says

(3.9)   (Well) why don't you come and have a spot of <u>lunch</u>?

The only thing new is *a spot of lunch; you coming* (= the *I going* of 3.2) and *having* are given since they are items that are recovered from the context.

The focus, now, is on only part of the information in the intonation unit; that which is new is narrowed down to *a spot of lunch*: hence narrow focus. Notice again that the tonic indicates the end of the new information. Thus, (3.9) illustrates – in the context of (3.2) – a narrow focus.

Then imagine the two people in conversation, in which the question of (3.3) is raised, about the destination of one person's holiday. After handling the response to that question, he or she may well return with the same question:

(3.10)   And where are you going on <u>your</u> holidays?

The only new item is *you/your*; *where*, *going* and *holidays* belong to the context so they are given. The focus is narrow; the tonic falls again at the end of the new information, in this case, a grammatical item. Notice that this phenomenon of placing the tonic on words like *your* and *you* is typical in situations where the second person asks the same question of the first person, e.g.:

(3.11)   (Good <u>mor</u>ning | how <u>are</u> you?)
            Very <u>well</u> | <u>thank</u> you | and how are <u>you</u>?

The answer to *Did you have a nice time?* (3.4) might possibly be:

(3.12)   We had an <u>aw</u>ful time

We having (= *you having* in (3.4)) and *time* are recoverable from the context, and only *awful* is new. Thus, the focus is narrow; indeed, very narrow, consisting solely of one word.

And a possible response to *Look at that man up there* (3.5) could be:

(3.13)   And look at <u>that</u> man

Again, the focus is narrow, confined to *that*, since all the other information is recoverable from the context supplied in (3.5).

In the above examples, you will notice that narrow focus necessarily assumes an element of given information. The focus itself involves new information which might be found either at the end of the intonation unit, or anywhere else. When narrow focus is located at the end of the intonation unit, as in (3.9), it happens to conform to neutral tonicity – the tonic accompanying the last lexical item. When narrow focus occurs elsewhere, it conforms to marked tonicity, since the tonic accompanies either a non-lexical item, as in (3.10), (3.11) and (3.13), or a non-final lexical item, as in (3.12). Thus, whereas broad focus will, of necessity, require neutral tonicity, narrow focus may happen to use neutral tonicity but is just as likely to involve marked tonicity.

So far, 'given' information has been identified with recoverability from the context. However, it could refer to anything that is visible, or known, in any situation. If we might return to the example of breaking apples in two, you could imagine a person actually doing this as their party piece; no other, linguistic, context would be necessary to contextualize the challenge:

(3.1d)   Can you break an apple in two?

The words *break*, *apple* and *two* do not need to have been uttered, but they are recoverable – not from the linguistic context, but from the physical situation.

In the narrative, (3.6), the speaker does not mention the word *drive* until he says:

– and this man | allowed his wife to drive the car

The last lexical item is *car*, but it has previously been mentioned and is therefore given; the next-to-last lexical item is *drive*, which has not been mentioned, but nevertheless the speaker still treats it as given. Why? The speaker obviously wants to narrow the focus of the information down to *wife*; he excludes *drive* from new information on the assumption that everybody knows that that is what you do with cars. *Drive* is implied; it is part of general knowledge, in the context of buying a new car. It is, thus, treated by the speaker as part of the given information in that intonation unit.

Given information is recoverable either from the linguistic context, the physical situation or general knowledge.

5. Marked tonicity

We have defined marked tonicity as the choice of tonicity that is not neutral. Neutral tonicity refers to the tonic accompanying the last (truly) lexical item in the intonation unit; marked tonicity typically takes two forms: the tonic accompanying a non-final lexical item or accompanying a grammatical item.

The main function of marked tonicity is to carry those cases of narrow focus that do not coincide with final lexical items, as in (3.10), (3.11), (3.12) and (3.13), and in (3.1b)–(3.1e). Contrast is an obvious case of narrow focus, as in the various renderings of (3.1). It emerges too in contrasts involving grammatical items. For instance, the neutral tonicity of (3.14a) can be contrasted in two, grammatical, ways:

(3.14a)   I have been asking for ages

(3.14b)   I have been asking for ages

which means something like 'It's not that I haven't been asking' – a contrast in affirmative/negative polarity; and

(3.14c)   I have been asking for ages

which means something like 'It's not that I'm now beginning to ask' – a contrast in tense.

It should not be too difficult to think of other contrasts involving grammatical items. Take pronouns, for example:

(3.15)   It's not what I think | but what you think

and prepositions:

(3.16)   Think of what you can put into it | not what you get out of it

and conjunctions:

(3.17)   Remember | I said if

and even morphemes:

(3.18)   That's what you're exporting | and we're importing

(3.19a)   She's an ex-girlfriend

as opposed to the normal

(3.19b)   She's an ex-girlfriend

We must be careful in dealing with compounds. Compounds are words composed, usually, of two otherwise independent words. To take a single example, *blackbird* is a compound consisting of two words that have an independent existence, *black* and *bird*. *Blackbird* is distinguished from a *black bird* in a number of ways: semantically, *blackbird* refers to a single concept, whereas *black bird* refers to two; grammatically, *blackbird* is unitary and cannot be divided, whereas *black bird* can be divided (*a black little bird*); orthographically, the compound is spelt as a single word, but the noun phrase as two separate words; and phonologically, *blackbird* has a single word stress, at the beginning, and *black bird* has two word stresses, one on each word. Compounds are thus distinguished semantically, grammatically, orthographically and phonologically from a parallel noun phrase. Unfortunately, the orthographical distinction is not consistent. The following compound can be spelt either as one word, two words, or hyphenated: *roadworks, road works, road-works*. It is when a compound is spelt as two words that a problem can arise in identifying neutral and marked tonicity; the spelling *road works* still represents a compound, as the word stress, grammar and semantics testify.

In the narrative we considered above, (3.6), *driveway* occurs as tonic; it is the final lexical item, which happens to be a compound, and is nowadays usually written as a single word. *Policeman* and *policewoman* are also examples of compounds normally written as single words, but the compound *police car* is usually still written as two words. So even if the written form of (3.20) has the compound as two words, it must be treated as a single lexical item:

(3.20)   And there goes the police car

And because the lexical item *police car* is final, (3.20) is a case of neutral tonicity, despite its written appearance.

However, the unstressed part of the compound would, occasionally, receive the tonic. Imagine a group of witnesses discussing an incident which involved the police and their vehicles and a dispute arises over a detail. One person might report that the ringleader of the group was taken away with the rest of the group in a police van; but another disputes this:

(3.21)   (A: He was taken with the rest of them in the po<u>lice</u> van

           B: No he <u>wasn't</u>)

           He was taken in the police <u>car</u>

This would be a case of marked tonicity because the normally unstressed element of the compound receives the tonic, rather like (3.18) and (3.19a) above.

Here are two more examples to illustrate tonicity and compounds. *Book case* can be written as *book case* and *book-case*, but the word stress is consistently on the first element. Thus (3.22) has neutral tonicity, despite the spelling:

(3.22)   What we need is a new <u>book</u> case

and (3.23) has marked tonicity, again despite the spelling:

(3.23)   He got a new <u>book</u> shelf | but what we need is a new book <u>case</u>

The compound *cheque book* is usually written as two words. (3.24) contains the compound in both neutral and marked tonicity:

(3.24)   I've lost my <u>cheque</u> book | It's not a single <u>cheque</u> | but the whole cheque <u>book</u>

Marked tonicity also emerges in other genres of spoken discourse, but not necessarily conveying contrast. It might simply be a way of avoiding a tonic on a repeated item. One genre familiar to many is the reading of football scores. If there is an outright victory, neutral tonicity prevails; but in the case of a draw, marked tonicity prevails. In (3.25)

(3.25)   Wales <u>three</u> | Belgium <u>one</u>

the scores themselves are the final lexical items in each of the intonation units: neutral tonicity. However (in the return match) in (3.26)

(3.26)   Belgium <u>one</u> | <u>Wales</u> one

the tonic is placed on *Wales*, because the score *one* is being repeated and treated as given. This is how all football followers can predict a draw before the announcer reaches the actual score in the second intonation unit.[6]

A second example is the announcement of telephone numbers. Most British numbers now have six or seven digits, and are usually uttered in two groups of three or four. If the final digit is identical to the final digit of the first group, it is treated as given; thus 751281 is usually rendered as

(3.27)   seven five <u>one</u> | two <u>eight</u> one

In the case of football scores and telephone numbers, marked tonicity does not represent contrast, but simply the avoidance of focusing on a repeated item.

Marked tonicity also occurs regularly in another class of clauses. When a clause ends in a common intransitive verb of motion or happening,[7] that verb – though it is the final lexical item – does not take the tonic. Consider the following examples:

(3.28)   The <u>doc</u>tor's coming

(3.29)   (Don't worry) <u>John's</u> going

(3.30)   An <u>ac</u>cident has happened

(3.31)   A <u>ques</u>tion was raised

(3.32)   Dis<u>cuss</u>ions took place

(3.33)   The <u>post</u>man called

The verbs *come* and *go* do not add anything of significance in (3.28) and (3.29), and they typically remain 'non-tonic' even when in final position. The verbs in the remaining examples are also relatively insignificant, because what you expect of accidents is that they happen, and what you expect of questions is that they are raised, and so on. The main information is *the doctor, John, an accident, a question, discussions, the postman*, and the following verb simply fills the obligatory slot of predicator. Linguists have often referred to the use of verbs in such cases as being semantically empty,[8] because they do not add extra information.

The cases stand in contrast to the usual neutral tonicity of examples with semantically richer words:

(3.34)   The doctor's <u>run</u>ning

(3.35)   (Don't worry) John's <u>eat</u>ing

(3.36)   An accident is being in<u>ves</u>tigated

(3.37)   A question was <u>an</u>swered

(3.38)   Discussions were an<u>nounced</u>

(3.39)   The postman <u>fell</u>

These verbs inform; they are not merely fillers.

6. The tonicity of final adjuncts

When adjuncts occur in the initial position of the clause, they gain semantic prominence, and like other classes of words become the (marked) theme of the clause. But when they occur at the end, they are often least prominent – but not always, and not all kinds either. The situation is a little more complicated, and a number of points need to be made.

The first point to be made is that certain verbs require adjuncts of place as their complements; verbs like *put, send* require a locative adjunct to complete their sense, e.g. you cannot just say *Put the books*, you have to add a locative element like *here* or *down*, etc. Thus a distinction needs to be kept between locatives as essential complements to verbs – they have got to be there – and locatives that add circumstantial information. Compare

(3.40)   The books are <u>here</u>

(3.41)   Put the books <u>here</u>

(3.42)   We've got some <u>books</u> here

In (3.40) and (3.41), *here* is complement to *are* and *put*, but in (3.42) it merely provides circumstantial information.

Circumstantial information is what adjuncts of place and time provide most of the time. If the adjuncts belong to closed systems like *here/there; now/then; yesterday/today/tomorrow*, they do not normally take the tonic, unless a contrast is intended. Compare a usual rendering with a contrastive rendering of the following:

(3.43a)   Let's <u>go</u> now

(3.43b)   Let's go <u>now</u> (as opposed to a time in the future)

(3.44a)   That's <u>all</u> for today

(3.44b)   That's all for to<u>day</u> (= 'you get more tomorrow')

(3.45a)   I saw <u>John</u> yesterday

(3.45b)   I saw John <u>yesterday</u> (as opposed to some other time)

(3.46a)   Let's <u>go</u> there

(3.46b)   Let's go <u>there</u> (as opposed to some other place)

There is another class of adjunct that acts in a similar 'non-tonic' way; they function as 'comment' adjuncts, as in the following examples:

(3.47)   I've never <u>read</u> it though

(3.48)   You must <u>read</u> it of course

(3.49)   He's not going to <u>read</u> it you know

(3.50)   They've already <u>read</u> it however

(3.51)   I've begun to <u>read</u> it at least

There are a number of such 'comment' adjuncts, but they operate in a fairly closed system and that is why they do not usually take the tonic. But like the time and place adjuncts, they **could** do – producing an emphatic, if not contrastive, effect, e.g.:

(3.48b)   You must read it of <u>course</u>

They seem to be more effective, though, in initial position:

(3.48c)   Of <u>course</u> you must read it

We have made two points so far: firstly, an adjunct, in some cases, is required as an essential complement to a verb, and in other cases, it provides circumstantial information, secondly, some adjuncts belong to quasi-grammatical closed systems, and if these happen to be in final position, they usually do not take the tonic. Other adjuncts, like adjuncts of manner, are lexical, i.e. they belong to open sets, and if they occur in final position are likely to take the tonic:

(3.52)   Let's go <u>quickly</u>

(3.53)   He read it very <u>well</u>

A third point relates to yet another possible rendering of final adjuncts; sometimes they can have an intonation unit all to themselves. For instance, we could say (3.43) as

(3.43c)   Let's <u>go</u> | <u>now</u>

with a falling tone on *go* and a slight rise on *now*. Compare also the following:

(3.44c)   That's <u>all</u> | for to<u>day</u>

(3.45c)   I saw <u>John</u> | <u>yes</u>terday

(3.42a)   We've got some <u>books</u> | <u>here</u>[9]

Strictly speaking, this is a matter of tonality, because an extra intonation unit has been created; but it affects tonicity, too, because the adverb necessarily becomes tonic in its own unit. We shall see, in the next chapter, that tone plays a significant role in these examples, too. But at this juncture all we need to note is that this pattern exists and that it gives more prominence to the adjunct than it would otherwise have. Compare, then:

(3.54a)   I don't <u>want</u> one now

with no prominence on *now*;

(3.54b)   I don't <u>want</u> one | <u>now</u>

with more prominence on *now*; and

(3.54c)   I don't want one <u>now</u>

with a great deal of prominence on *now*, suggesting a contrast with a point of time in the future.

This threefold system of prominence operates with adjuncts of place and comment, too. It also operates with another class of adjuncts, those that indicate viewpoints. Compare the viewpoint adjunct, *economically*, in these examples:

(3.55a)   We're in poor <u>shape</u> economically

(3.55b)   We're in poor <u>shape</u> | eco<u>no</u>mically

(3.55c)   We're in poor shape eco<u>no</u>mically

Incidentally, a similar, but twofold, system of prominence operates with final vocatives:

(3.56a)   They're <u>here</u> John

(3.56b)   They're <u>here</u> | <u>John</u>

with final glosses.

(3.57a)   He shouldn't have <u>done</u> it the fool

(3.57b)   He shouldn't have <u>done</u> it | the <u>fool</u>

and with final direct speech markers:

(3.58a)   Don't <u>run</u> he said

(3.58b)   Don't <u>run</u> | he <u>said</u>

The effect of the extra intonation unit containing the final vocative, gloss or direct speech marker is to give a little more prominence to the item concerned.

A fourth point can now be made: some adjuncts can have two different functions, and the different functions follow different tonicity patterns. An adjunct like *normally* or *frankly* can be used as an adjunct of manner, and if it comes at the end of its clause, as in the following examples, it would tend to be accompanied by the tonic:

(3.59a)   He <u>nor</u>mally (i.e. in a normal manner)

(3.60a)   I couldn't speak to him <u>frank</u>ly (i.e. in a frank manner)

This is the pattern we would expect as in the other cases of manner we have seen ((3.52), (3.53)).

But *normally* and *frankly* can also act as comment adjuncts, and as is typical of comment adjuncts, they do not take the tonic:

(3.59b)   He <u>drives</u> normally (i.e. it is normal for him to drive)

(3.60b)   I couldn't <u>speak</u> to him frankly ('I have to be frank, I ...')

Other comment adjuncts include *fortunately, unfortunately, thankfully, happily*, etc., and follow the same pattern for that function. An alternative rendering to (3.59b) and (3.60b) is to grant the comment adjuncts their own intonation unit to give them greater prominence, following the pattern of final adjuncts described above:

(3.59c)   He <u>drives</u> | <u>nor</u>mally

(3.60c)   I couldn't <u>speak</u> to him | <u>frank</u>ly

with a falling tone on the first tonic, and a rising tone on the second.

7. Tonicity by default

So far, we have maintained a distinction between neutral and marked tonicity depending on the position of the tonic within a given unit of intonation. Neutral tonicity indicates broad focus where all the information in the unit is new, but it may also indicate narrow focus if that which is new information is found at the end of the unit. Marked tonicity indicates new information that is either grammatical or not final.

We have also pointed out the oddity of cases like (3.8)

(3.8)   You'd love to attend the <u>next</u> one!?

which was an echo of (3.7)

(3.7)   I'd love to attend the <u>next</u> one.

An echo is an identical wording of a part of, or the whole of, a previous utterance, usually for the sake of expressing disbelief or surprise, or checking against mishearing. Here are two more examples:

(3.61)   (A: Jonathan won his <u>race</u>!)
           B: He <u>won</u>

(3.62)   (A: It costs eighty-three <u>pounds</u>)
           B: Eighty-three <u>pounds</u> did you say

A similar case is when a person responds to a request for a repetition, e.g.:

(3.63)   (A: Is this your <u>hand</u>bag)
           (B: <u>Par</u>don)

           A: Is this your <u>hand</u>bag

Strictly speaking, in all these cases of echoes and repetitions, the intonation unit only consists of given information, but the units are treated as if they contain the same information structure of given and new as the original. But there are two other cases where an intonation unit only consists of given information: one is where the given information is the point of contrast. Consider this example:

(3.64)   Tom, Dick and Harry all got <u>firsts</u> | but <u>Tom</u> | was given the <u>prize</u>

The middle unit only contains given information, but it is now the point of contrast. In (3.65), the second unit again contains only given information, but the information is different, and is again contrastive:

(3.65)   I see the <u>moon</u> | and the moon sees <u>me</u>

The second case of all-given information is 'insists', as Cruttenden (1986: 93-4) calls them. Here are some examples:

(3.66)   (A: Why have you invited the Robinsons?)
            B: But I <u>have</u>n't invited them!

(3.67)   (A: How many <u>tea bags</u> did you use?)
            B: I don't <u>use</u> tea bags

(3.68)   (A: Has John read Slaughterhouse <u>Five</u>?)
            B: <u>No</u> | John doesn't <u>read</u> books

All of B's replies are 'insists'; B insists that A's presuppositions are not valid, but note that B's counter-presuppositional 'insists' only contain information that is given. Furthermore, B focuses on what he or she assumes to be the basis of A's presupposition and then negates it. The focus in the 'insists' usually correlates, therefore, with the given information in the original, because it is the given information in the original that is the basis of A's presupposition.

We can thus explain the focus of these cases of all-given intonation units, but there is one, final, case, which is much more difficult to explain.

In a radio programme about Edwardian days and ways in London, a person was asked what they could remember about those days. The reply came as:

(3.69)   I don't know that there is anything <u>to</u> remember

Everything was treated as given, but why would the infinitive marker *to* receive the tonic when it has absolutely no meaning of its own? We cannot dismiss it as a 'rogue' rendering, nor as a dialectal variation, since many odd cases like this crop up.[10]

The explanation seems to be that the speaker is countering the whole presupposition of the original question. In order to do this, he (it was a man!) could not 'afford' to put the tonic on a lexical item in case he gave undue prominence to it and made it sound contrastive; the *anything* is the given equivalent of the *what* of the original question, and he seemed to want to avoid giving that prominence too. What he did, therefore, was to seek the least semantically significant item in the unit and place the tonic there, in order to avoid narrow focus and the possible interpretation of contrastivity. In order to indicate a 'broad' focus in all-given information, the tonic gets placed on the least semantically significant item towards the end of the unit. This is a genuine case of tonicity placement by default – avoiding all the other potentially misleading options.

To illustrate tonicity by default further, we will take an example from Cruttenden (1986: 93):

(3.70)   They're not very <u>expert</u> | but there are lots <u>of</u> them

In this case, the speaker could have chosen to place the tonic in the second unit on *lots* as the most lexical item, and this would have sounded quite satisfactory. However, *lots* is treated as given in (3.70), and the speaker wishes to avoid an interpretation of contrastivity in *are* and *them*, and so the tonic gets placed on the least semantically significant item towards the end of the unit, thus, by default, on *of*.

Some linguists[11] treat all the cases presented in this section as cases of default, but it seems to me that genuine cases of tonicity by default are those cases where a speaker – as in (3.69) and (3.70) – places the tonic on the last item of zero significance in the unit, in the deliberate attempt to avoid potentially misleading interpretations of narrow focus.

8. Tonicity and grammar

Finally in this chapter, we consider a few cases where tonicity realizes a syntactic contrast in parallel wording, in the same way as tonality occasionally does.

One example was given in Chapter 1: the difference between

(1.22)   He <u>asked</u> himself

(1.23)   He asked him<u>self</u>

The explanation was given as a syntactic contrast between the reflexive and the emphatic pronouns, which also affected the transitivity of the verb: *asked* in (1.22) is transitive, in (1.23) it is intransitive. Here is another example with the same explanation:

(3.71)   I have never <u>taught</u> myself

(3.72)   I have never taught my<u>self</u>

A similar example can be found with the verb *feel*.[12] In (3.73), we have an example of a reflexive pronoun complementing a transitive verb, as in (3.71) and (1.22):

(3.73)   He <u>felt</u> himself (e.g. to see if he was bruised)

The tonicity is neutral in these cases because the tonic accompanies the last lexical item. The marked version, (3.74), in this case does not indicate an emphatic pronoun (as in (3.72) and (1.23)), but an intensive complement to an intransitive verb:

(3.74)   He felt him<u>self</u> (i.e. he felt much more like his usual self)

70

This version parallels other intensive complements as in *He felt good, He felt embarrassed*, etc., where the tonic would usually accompany the complement itself.

A second example of tonicity contrast in syntax is provided by the following pair:

(3.75)   Shoot John

(3.76)   Shoot John

In (3.75), *John* is a final vocative, which typically is left 'non-tonic' (although, as we have seen above, (3.57b), it could have its own intonation unit if the speaker wished to give the vocative more prominence). In the written mode, it would be preceded by a comma, but as we have often pointed out, commas belong to the **written** mode only, whereas in the spoken mode, we have to rely on intonation. (3.76) manifests neutral tonicity, with *John* as direct object complementing the transitive use of the verb *shoot*. You will now have noticed a number of cases where intonation plays a specific role in distinguishing transitive and intransitive uses of the same verb.

The third example has already been dealt with above, in the section on tonicity and final adjuncts; it will simply be mentioned again here to complete the picture of tonicity contrasts in syntax. Adjuncts like *normally, frankly, stupidly, happily* can function as comment adjuncts as well as adjuncts of manner. When they occur in final position in a clause, they are potentially ambiguous; in the written mode, the ambiguity is usually resolved by the presence or absence of a comma preceding them, but in the spoken mode, we have to rely on intonation. Two further pairs can illustrate the distinction; in each pair, the first item has neutral tonicity with the tonic accompanying the adjunct of manner; the second pair has marked tonicity with the tonic accompanying another item.

(3.77a)   They didn't come happily (i.e. not in a happy mood)

(3.77b)   They didn't come happily (i.e. 'I am happy to say that ...')

(3.78a)   He presented me with the same information stupidly (i.e. in a stupid manner)

(3.78b)   He presented me with the same information stupidly (i.e. 'It was stupid of him to ...')

We have now comprehensively reviewed the system of tonicity in English intonation. Now check through the narrative of (3.6) and see if you can explain the tonicity in each intonation unit; this chapter has covered all the possibilities.

Here is an example of a tonicity exercise from a course in practising English as a foreign language;[13] see if you can supply all the necessary explanations. Each of the sentences overleaf is capable of being completed in a number of different ways. The written form does not help, but the spoken form would, by having the tonic syllable on the most appropriate word (or words). For each of the continuations, which word(s) in the original would have to have been tonic?

I can't see very well with my glasses now ...
(a) but John can
(b) but I can see well with yours
(c) but I can see quite well
(d) but I could when I bought them
(e) but John can see well with his
(f) but I can see well if I don't wear them

John's brother tried to buy both of the books ...
(a) not to borrow them
(b) not the magazines
(c) but he wasn't able to
(d) but one book had been sold

The early lenses weren't made of glass ...
(a) but the later ones were
(b) although some of the early windows were
(c) although many people think they were
(d) they were made of crystal

John finds it very difficult to wear contact lenses ...
(a) and so does Bill
(b) but Bill doesn't
(c) but Mary finds it easy
(d) but he has no difficulty in wearing spectacles

Notes

1. For a full discussion, see Wells (1986) and Tench (1990: 201–14).
2. Wells (1986: 57) maintains that kinetic tone is **invariably** present; however, we must allow for the existence of (so-called) level tones.
3. The semantic and grammatical clues to identifying the tonic, and therefore the focus of intonation, are described in detail in Taglicht (1984).
4. Taken from Allen (1954).
5. See Tench (1990: 513) for further discussion and the one possible exception.
6. This has traditionally been the case on radio; television has begun to affect the intonation of football result announcements, because the scores are presented on screen before the announcement.
7. Cruttenden (1986: 83–4) calls such clauses 'event sentences'.
8. Bolinger (1986: 120–3). Halliday (1967: 38) also noted 'certain high frequency collocations' in intransitive clauses, e.g. *My head aches; The door's locked;* but this is essentially the same phenomenon.
9. NB this pattern does not work with (3.41): *Put the books | here,* where the locative element is complement to the verb.
10. See Cruttenden (1986: 93) and Ladd (1980: 81) for similar cases.
11. E.g. Ladd (1980).
12. This example is taken directly from Halliday (1967: 39).
13. Taken from Dickinson and Mackin (1969: 28–9).

4

TONES

THE TUNES OF INTONATION

---

1. Primary and secondary tones

It is the **tones** of English intonation that most people are aware of. It should by now be clear that English intonation comprises three separate, though related, systems: tonality (intonation units), tonicity (the tonic syllables) and tone. But people are much more aware of the third system than they are of tonality or even tonicity. Tone refers to pitch movements, and that observation which has frequently been commented on – 'that it is not what they said, but the way they said it' – relies primarily upon the pitch movements. We are aware of rises and falls of pitch and high levels, low levels, 'bouncing' movements, calling tones and so on, which all contribute to a wide range of different meanings.

Tone has been defined hitherto as the contrastive pitch movement on the tonic syllable; so, for instance, in the standard example we took in Chapter 1, the tone of

(1.10)   A dog is a man's best <u>friend</u>

is the falling tone on the tonic, *friend*. We now need to make a further distinction, because it is obvious that there are other pitch movements besides that which occurs on the tonic syllable. We make a distinction between primary and secondary tones. **Primary** tones are the basic contrastive pitch movements on the tonic, i.e. whether the pitch of the voice moves up (rises), or moves down (falls), or combines a movement of down and then up (fall-rises). **Secondary** tones are the finer distinctions of the primary tones, i.e. the **degree** to which the pitch of the voice rises, falls or combines a fall and a rise – whether there is, for example, a rise to a high pitch or a mid pitch, or a fall from a mid pitch or a high pitch, etc. Secondary tones also cover the pitch movements in the pre-tonic segment (the head and the pre-head). (Pitch movements in the tail are not considered separately from

73

the pitch on the tonic because they are an extension to the tone itself.)

The primary tones of English, i.e. the fall, the rise and the fall-rise, function, like tonality and tonicity, in the organization of information, but they also feature, like the other systems, in a second function. Whereas tonality and tonicity produce contrasts in grammar, the tone system produces contrasts in the communicative, or illocutionary, function; that is, they help to indicate differences between telling and asking, between commanding and requesting, between congratulating and wishing, and a whole host of similar functions that language is used to fulfil

The secondary tones do not function, as such, in the organization of information – or, for that matter, in either grammar or the communicative functions. Their role is in the expression of attitudes, and the next chapter will be devoted to a full description of all the possible pitch variations that are discernible in English.

In this chapter we will concentrate on the role of the primary tones; we will consider, first, their role in the organization of information and then their role in the communicative functions. But even before we consider these roles, it would first of all be as well to look at some of their characteristic patterns of pitch.

2. Primary tones: falls, rises and fall-rises

We come now to the details of the pitch movements. One point must be made clear: pitch is a relative matter. We do not talk about absolute pitch as one might in music, but rather about levels and movements of pitch within an individual's range of voice. An obvious example is that the actual range of pitch of most adults is lower than that of children, and again, the actual range of pitch of men is, on average, lower than that of women. In other words, in absolute, musical, terms a low level of pitch for a child might in actual fact be higher than a high level of a man's. The child's low level of pitch is measured within the 'scale' of the child's full range of pitch, and the man's high pitch is measured within the 'scale' of the man's range.

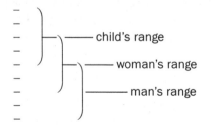

It is quite useful to think of your own range of pitch as having what you might call a high level, a low level and a mid level; it should also be possible

to imagine an intermediate range of pitch between high and mid, and another between mid and low. These intermediate ranges could also be thought of as having a notional midway point between high and mid and between mid and low; this would provide a kind of five-point 'scale':

high

mid-high

mid

mid-low

low

Experiment with a word like *No* or *Well* and try and establish, at least, a high, a mid and a low variety, keeping the pitch fairly steady. If you now say *No* as a response to a question, the most natural way of intoning it would be for it to be accompanied by a pitch movement falling from about mid-high (or mid) to mid-low (or low). There are, of course, very many different ways of responding with *No*, but the pitch movement just described could be considered as the most normal or ordinary. This pitch movement is known as the neutral fall, because no other meaning or connotation is added to that of 'plain statement'. It is the pitch you would expect if no other meaning or connotation was intended. It is indicated by a downward-pointing line before the syllable concerned.

2.1 Falls

The neutral fall can be contrasted with a high fall, in which the beginning point is much higher. This sounds like a stronger, more determined response; the symbol is placed higher. Compare (4.1) and (4.2):

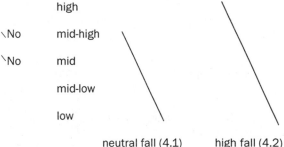

		high
(4.1)	\No	mid-high
(4.2)	ʼNo	mid
		mid-low
		low

neutral fall (4.1)   high fall (4.2)

Furthermore, the neutral fall can be contrasted with a low fall, in which the beginning point is about mid-low, and the pitch drops to low. The symbol is placed lower, and its meaning is something like mild or expected:

(4.3) ⟍No

high
mid-high
mid
mid-low
low

low fall (4.3)

Compare all three. Remember that it is the neutral fall that is the primary tone, and the high and low varieties are secondary tones. There are 'primary' functions associated with the fall, but 'secondary' – attitudinal – functions associated with the alternative degrees of fall.

If you take an example with a tail, you will find that there are two possible ways of distributing the fall over the syllables: either the main drop of the fall is carried through the tonic syllable, and then the unstressed syllable(s) will carry it on to its final pitch level; or the tonic syllable keeps a fairly high pitch and the fall is executed by a sudden drop to the low pitch in the following syllable(s). Compare (4.4a) and (4.4b):

(4.4a)   Never   (4.4b)   Never

There is no difference in meaning, and so both can be symbolized as

(4.4) ⟍Never

There are, obviously, high and low varieties of a fall on a word like *never*:

(4.5) ⟍Never

(4.6) ⟍Never

The (b) variety of the fall is quite likely to accompany the high fall. It is also quite likely to accompany any tonic syllable that has a short vowel and a voiceless consonant, as in *nothing* .

Let us now take an example with a pre-tonic segment, e.g.:

(4.7) I don't be⟍lieve it

The tonic syllable is the second syllable of *believe*; in a prepared intonational transcription, a gap is left before the tonic syllable for the intonation symbol to be inserted, as above. Otherwise, the symbol is placed through the letters: *believe*. (4.7) can be rendered with a high fall (4.8) and low fall (4.9):

(4.8) I don't be⟍lieve it

(4.9) I don't be⟍lieve it

with the same additional connotations as with (4.2) and (4.3).

One of the most difficult tasks in intonation analysis is to discern the pitch movement on the tonic syllable itself. In each of the renderings of *I don't believe it above*, the pitch level of the unstressed syllable *he-* before the tonic *-lieve* is likely to be fairly low. The pitch of the voice has then to jump up to a higher level in order to effect a fall – you can't fall to low if you are at low already! This inevitable jump up is often considered by the novice to be a rise, and so a complete misconception can take place in the novice's mind as to what tone is actually being performed. This gives rise to the fairly familiar complaint that 'I can't tell the difference between a fall and a rise'. What you must try and do is concentrate on the pitch movement of the tonic itself and separate it in your mind from any preceding words or syllables. This, however, is quite awkward when one or more syllables of a single word belong to the pre-tonic and another syllable belongs to the tonic. The way to do it is to first of all determine what the tonic syllable is, and any following syllables, and then to imitate the pitch movement of that syllable; and practice makes perfect. If there are any following syllables in a tail, they give you a very valuable clue: if the tail remains low pitched, then the tone must have fallen; if the tail is relatively high, then the tone must have risen.

2.2 Rises

We will now turn to the case of rising tones. Obviously, the beginning point is low (or mid-low); then the pitch rises to mid or mid-high. (4.10) sounds a little like a query, or possibly the beginning of a response which the speaker is going to extend, like *No, I don't think so*

```
                    high
                    mid-high          /
(4.10)      /No     mid              /
                    mid-low         /
                    low            /
```

neutral rise (4.10)

The symbol is an upward-pointing line before the syllable concerned; it might be tempting to add a question mark (?) to *No*, but as in the above explanation, a rise can also indicate something like 'This is not all I want to say; I'm going to continue', in which case it might be tempting to add a comma (,). It is best to resist such temptations since punctuation is a feature of the written mode, and whereas it does correspond to a certain extent to intonation, it is by no means as sophisticated.[1]

The rising tone as described above is its neutral form. Like the fall, it has high and low varieties, depending on the extent of the rise.[2] The high rise is commonly associated with a stronger sense of querying, suggesting surprise or even disbelief:

77

(4.11)   ′No

The rise finishes at a high point. The low rise finishes at about mid-low and suggests a non-committal, or even grumbling, attitude:

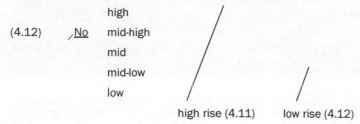

	high
(4.12) ,No	mid-high
	mid
	mid-low
	low

high rise (4.11)   low rise (4.12)

The neutral, high and low rises may accompany tonics and tails, with the same range of meanings: compare

(4.13)   ∕Never

(4.14)   ′Never

(4.15)   ,Never

The rise requires a low starting-point and the main difference between the three varieties is the end point of the rise in the tail. There is an (a) and (b) form as in the fall, which is heard best in the high rise:

(4.14a)   ∕   (4.14b)   ⌐
          Never   Never

The (b) form would also be quite likely in cases of tonic syllables containing a short vowel, with a voiceless consonant following.

The rise can also be demonstrated in an example with a pre-tonic segment:

(4.16)   Do you really be∕lieve it

The symbol comes in the middle of the word again, immediately before the tonic syllable. It has a high variety:

(4.17)   Do you really be′lieve it

with the same meaning, of course, as in (4.11): and a low variety:

(4.18)   Do you really be,lieve it

with a meaning parallel to that of (4.12).

Once again, there is a difficulty in the task of discerning the rise in the tonic syllable, because in order to effect the rise, the pitch of the voice must drop after *be-* to low so that the rise can begin. As with falls, the novice is likely to think that this drop is part of the tone, but the same kind of advice must be taken in the case of rises, too. If there is a tail, that is a valuable clue, since if there has been a rise, the tail will finish relatively high itself.

2.3 Fall-rises

Finally, we turn to fall-rise tones, which comprise a sequence of a fall and a rise even within a single syllable. ∨No said in this way means something like 'I disagree, but there's more to think about'; colloquially, it is often preceded by *Well* to help reduce the sense of total disagreement. The symbol for the fall-rise is ∨, a combination of the fall and the rise symbols, and the pitch pattern looks something like:

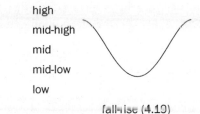

		high
		mid-high
(4.19)	∨No	mid
		mid-low
		low

fall-rise (4.19)

With a tail, as in *Never*, there is again an (a) and a (b) form:

(4.20a)   Never   (4.20b)   Never

but a single means of symbolizing them: ∨<u>Ne</u>ver

The first, stressed, syllable remains the most prominent and is thus identified as the tonic, but the fall-rise movement is spread over the whole tonic segment (i.e. tonic + tail). The 'distance' between the fall and the rise elements is increased the longer the tail is. If (4.21) is said with a fall-rise tone accompanying the tonic syllable *I* (meaning 'As far as I am concerned, in contrast to what others may think'), the fall accompanies the tonic syllable *I* and the rise is delayed until the final stressed syllable of the tail, producing a kind of 'split' fall-rise:

(4.21)   ∨<u>I</u> don't believe it

<u>I</u> don't believe it

The fall-rise movement is spread over the whole of the tonic segment; the rise is split off from the fall and accompanies either the final stressed syllable, or if there is not one, the final unstressed syllable. Here is another example of a split fall-rise, with stressed syllables in the tail:

(4.22)   I don't ∨ <u>want</u> to have to think about it

(I don't) want to have to think about it

and another example of split fall-rise, with no stressed syllables in the tail:

(4.23)   Un∨<u>for</u>tunately

(Un)fortunately

79

3. Tones and the status of information

We have seen that when a speaker says something, they have to manage the organization of information. This management entails the division of the whole information into separate, consecutive pieces, which are represented in speech by units of intonation (tonality): secondly, it entails the realization of focus, either broad or narrow, in terms of new and given information, which is all represented in speech by a choice in the placement of the tonic syllable (tonicity); and now, thirdly, we shall see that the management of the organization of information entails the recognition of a status accorded to each piece of information, which is represented in speech by choices in the tone system.

Halliday is the linguist who has drawn most attention to this phenomenon, although he never used the term 'status'. He referred to 'major' and 'minor' information (Halliday, 1967: 37) and various kinds of dependence that one unit of information might have on another (ibid.: 34–5).[3]

3.1 Falls and rises

We noted above that one possible meaning of the rising tone is 'This is not all I want to say; I'm going to continue'. There is widespread agreement to this sense of information not yet being completed.[4] One function of the rise, then, is to indicate 'incomplete information'.

A common sequence of tones in a pair of intonation units is a rise in the first, to indicate incompleteness, followed by a fall in the second, to indicate completeness, e.g.:

(4.24)   He simply got ⁄<u>up</u> | and went ＼ <u>home</u>

If you say the first unit of (4.24) with a rise, your listener will expect you to continue; if you don't continue, the information will certainly sound incomplete, left, as it were, 'hanging in the air'.

Another common sequence of tones in a pair of intonation units is the reverse: a fall in the first, and a rise in the second. In this case, the rise cannot mean incomplete, because it does in fact come at the end, e.g.:

(4.25)   But he didn't go to ＼<u>bed</u> | though he was ⁄<u>tired</u>

This sequence is what Halliday termed **major** and **minor** information. The main piece of information is contained in the first unit, and the second unit contains an extra piece of information; in the speaker's perception of the message, not going to bed is treated as the major piece of information, with reference to tiredness as minor, representing merely circumstantial information.

We cannot label the fall, therefore, as necessarily indicating complete information, since that is not the case in (4.25), even though it is in (4.24).

Major/minor is one system in information; complete/incomplete is another: a fall represents either major or complete and a rise either minor or incomplete. One suggestion is to combine the status of major and complete into a single category of 'primary information', and to combine minor and incomplete into a single category of 'secondary information'. There is a slight problem with this otherwise neat solution: there is a variation to the rising tone in incomplete information that is not available in minor information.

The variation to the rising tone indicating incomplete information is that instead of a rising pitch on the tonic syllable there could be a slight jump up to a mid-pitched level tone. If you count to four, you may either have a rising tone on each of the first three numbers (and a fall on *four*) or you may keep a mid-level pitch on each of the first three, symbolized in (4.26b) by a horizontal line at mid level:

(4.26a)   /one | /two | /three | \four

(4.26b)   –one | –two | –three | \four

This alternative type of rise, strictly speaking, runs counter to the definition of tones given so far, in that there is no movement of pitch. However, its existence is attested not only by Halliday, but by others too.[5] It is recognized here as a tone on secondary evidence: that it occurs on the tonic syllable, and that it is an alternative to a variety that fully conforms with the definition.

This mid-level variety only occurs in a non-final unit of intonation; and it is used as an alternative to the true rise to indicate incomplete information. This is why intonation analysts are reluctant to consider incomplete and minor information as a single category.

Notice that in both varieties of (4.26), the rise, or the mid-level tone, indicates that the counting is incomplete, and that the fall indicates that it is complete. (If you were counting to five, then *four* would have an indication of incomplete, of course, and *five* would take the fall.) This is how we intone lists, e.g.:

(4.27)   I lost my /passport | my /tickets | my /money | and the letter
          for Mr \Tan

Notice how the mid-level tone is often used to indicate misfortune:

(4.28)   I lost my –passport | my –tickets | my –money | that letter |
          the \lot

The mid-level tone may possibly establish itself as a separate contrasting tone, say in another generation's time, in which case we would have to revise the description of English intonation. Just as the pronunciation of consonants, vowels and word stress changes over a period of time, intonation also gradually changes, and we may well be witnessing a change in this respect, especially as the older intonation descriptions, like

Armstrong and Ward (1926) and Palmer (1922), did not include reference to a mid-level tone at all.

We can now recap. In a close sequence of intonation units, a rise indicates either incomplete or minor information, depending on whether it precedes or follows the fall. You will also recall examples from Chapter 3, in which a final adjunct can either be contained in the intonation unit of the clause preceding it, or it can have its own unit. In the latter case, the adjunct will typically take a rise, as minor, circumstantial information; see, for example, the following from Chapter 3:[6]

(3.42a)   We've got some \\<u>books</u> | /<u>here</u>

(3.43c)   Let's \\<u>go</u> | /<u>now</u>

(3.44c)   That's \\<u>all</u> | for to/<u>day</u>

(3.45c)   I saw \\<u>John</u> | /<u>yester</u>day (or: yester/<u>day</u>)

(3.55b)   We're in poor \\<u>shape</u> | eco/<u>no</u>mically

(3.56b)   They're \\<u>here</u> | /<u>John</u>

(3.57b)   He shouldn't have \\<u>done</u> it | the /<u>fool</u>

(3.58b)   Don't \\<u>run</u> | he /<u>said</u>

(3.59c)   He \\<u>drives</u> | /<u>normally</u>

(3.60c)   I couldn't \\<u>speak</u> to him | /<u>frankly</u>

A problem of identification may well have occurred to you: how can you tell the difference between a sequence of fall-plus-rise, as in the above, and a split fall-rise that is spread over a number of syllables? Some cases of the fall-rise tone are not problematical: if the pitch movement is contained in a single syllable, it is a single tone, not a sequence of two: if the pitch movement has a rise on a final unstressed syllable, it is the single fall-rise tone, because the rise in the fall-plus-rise sequence would have to co-occur with a tonic, i.e. stressed syllable. The problem arises when the rise occurs on a stressed syllable: is it the second tonic in the fall-plus-rise sequence or is it the rise component of a split fall-rise? The phonetic answer may not seem too helpful at first to a novice: a single fall-rise tone has only one tonic syllable and the rise component ends at a high level: the fall-plus-rise sequence has two tonics and the rise ends at approximately mid level. The semantic answer may be more helpful: the fall-rise tone relates to one piece of information in one intonation unit, whereas the fall-plus-rise sequence relates to two pieces of information in two intonation units. The question to ask, therefore, is: does the rise element constitute the kind of information that can be described as circumstantial? For example, in (4.21), the rise element occurs with *believe it*: that cannot be considered, syntactically, as circumstantial information, because it is the main verb: but what about (4.22)?

The original (4.22) was given as an instance of a single fall-rise tone, which in this case signified something like 'Whereas I don't want to have to think about it, it looks as if I shall have to, against my wishes'

(4.22)   I don't ∨<u>want</u> to have to think about it

The rise component ends high. In

(4.29)   I don't \<u>want</u> | to have to /<u>think</u> about it

the rise ends in approximately the mid level: the second unit is minor information compared to the major information in the first: it means something like 'Thinking about it is not what I want to do'.

3.2   Fall-rises

It is time now to look more precisely at the meanings of the fall-rise, and as in the case of the rising tone, the fall-rise has different meanings depending on whether it precedes a fall, or whether it itself is final.

When a fall-rise tone precedes a fall in a close sequence of two units, it comes as a contrast with the ordinary rise. Compare (4.30), with a rise simply indicating incompleteness, with (4.31), with a fall-rise:

(4.30)   In the /<u>kitchen</u> | you'll find a sur\<u>prise</u>

(4.31)   In the ∨<u>kitchen</u> | you'll find a sur\<u>prise</u>

(4.30) and (4.31) represent a typical case of marked theme (see Chapter 2, p. 37), but whereas the rise in (4.30) merely leads on to the major information, the fall-rise in (4.31) highlights the theme itself. The non-final fall-rise has this effect on the theme of a clause – it **highlights** it. Here is another pair of examples:

(4.32)   Un/<u>fortunately</u> | he can't \<u>come</u>

(4.33)   Un∨<u>fortunately</u> | he can't \<u>come</u>

The rise in (4.32) merely acts as a means of connecting the comment adjunct as theme to the remainder of the clause; in (4.33), the fall-rise draws attention specifically to the comment adjunct itself – it is no longer merely a connective, it is a comment in its own right and obviously gives expression to some thought in the speaker's mind (and if we knew, or invented, a context, we could speculate on what that thought might be).

This use of the fall-rise is not restricted to cases of marked theme, however; its use highlights cases of neutral theme too:

(4.34)   ∨<u>I</u> | \<u>can</u> come

(4.35)   My ∨<u>brother</u> | wouldn't even \<u>dream</u> of it

In these examples, the clause subjects are the themes, and a speaker can highlight them, if desired, by separating them off as a separate intonation unit from the unit containing the predicate. Thus a message in both cases is managed as two, separate, pieces of information – theme and rheme, but with the theme specially highlighted.

A whole clause can act as theme, when it precedes another; the first theme is usually subordinate to the second, independent, one.[7] Take (4.36) as an example:

(4.36)   If she /comes | that'll make \five of us

A speaker could highlight the theme with a fall-rise:

(4.37)   If she ˅comes | that'll make \five of us

or even

(4.38)   ˅If she comes | that'll make \five of us

In (4.38), the *If* is particularly highlighted. (Notice that the fall occurs on the tonic *If* and the rise component is delayed until the (final) stressed syllable: in this case, *comes*.)

And now we consider the use of the fall-rise in final position. It is generally agreed[8] that such uses of the fall-rise indicate some kind of **implication**. Halliday once glossed the meaning as 'there is a *but* about it' (Halliday, 1967: 27); he extended the meanings to include reservation, contrast, personal opinion offered for consideration, and concession (Halliday, 1970: 26–8). Here are some examples:

(4.39)   It's ˅cheap (reservation: 'but that's not the only thing that is true about it')

(4.40)   It ˅looks expensive (contrast: 'but is it really?')

(4.41)   It's worth con˅sidering (personal opinion: 'that's what I think')

(4.42)   Let him ˅think about it (concession: 'at least, do that')

All of these examples can be summed up for convenience under the term 'implication'. Kingdon (1958: 59–60) expressed it thus: the fall-rise conveys 'some insinuation in making the statement, expecting [the] hearer to understand more than is said'. The speaker does not have to verbalize the insinuation, but assumes that the hearer can extrapolate the additional message from the context, the setting or common knowledge. For instance, if a person in a coffee shop says

(4.43)   I don't ˅like coffee

the implication might be 'I don't know why you brought me here', or 'Although I don't like coffee, I'll show willing and drink some', or 'Do you think they offer an alternative drink?', and so on; the speaker expects the hearer to interpret the utterance correctly from whatever clues the speaker thinks the hearer has. The point of using the fall-rise is that the additional thought does not need to be expressed overtly.

We noted in Chapter 2, p. 46, a contrast in tonality between

(2.72a)   I didn't <u>come</u> | because he <u>told</u> me

and

(2.72b)   I didn't come because he <u>told</u> me

and in a similar pair:

(2.73a)   He didn't <u>go</u> | so that he could get pro<u>mo</u>tion

and

(2.73b)   He didn't go so that he could get pro<u>mo</u>tion

We remarked then that the negativization of the reason in (2.72b) and of the result in (2.73b) implied some other, unspecified, reason and result. They would both be quite naturally rendered with a fall-rise on the tonic:

(2.72b)   I didn't come because he ∨<u>told</u> me
           (implication: 'I came for another reason')

(2.73b)   He didn't go so that he could get pro∨<u>mo</u>tion
           (implication: 'he went with another expectation')

Finally, a well-known example of a contrast between a fall and a fall-rise associated with *any*-words, which was first raised by Lee (1956: 347). Compare

(4.44)   They don't admit \\<u>any</u> students

with

(4.45)   They don't admit ∨<u>any</u> students

The clear meaning of (4.44) is that all students are excluded, but what is the implication of (4.45)? It is that some students **are** admitted; the implication might even be that students who can be admitted are special in some way. See if you can work out the implications of the following:

(4.46)   He doesn't compose his songs just ∨<u>any</u>where

(4.47)   He doesn't sing to ∨<u>any</u>one

(4.48)   He doesn't present them ∨<u>any</u> how (or: ∨<u>any</u> old how)

(4.49)   He doesn't write ∨<u>any</u>thing

(4.50)   He doesn't do it ∨<u>any</u> time

(4.51)   He doesn't go ∨<u>any</u>way

The implications in each case refer to certain specific or even special places, people, ways, things and times.

We are now ready to sum up the choices in the tone system for the indication of information status. A rising tone before a fall indicates incomplete information; after a fall, minor information. A falling-rising tone before a fall indicates theme highlighting; after a fall, or independently, it indicates an implication, an unspoken message that the hearer is expected to interpret. A falling tone indicates major information, whether it is preceded or followed by either a rise or fall-rise. In some respects it acts as a **dominant** tone, which can be **satellited** by other tones. The system is therefore:

```
                          ┌─ major: \
                          ├─ minor: / (in final position)
status of information ────┼─ incomplete: / (in non final position)
                          ├─ implication: v (in final position)
                          └─ theme highlighted: v (in non-final position)
```

and is illustrated as follows:

(4.52)   It's suddenly become very \<u>cold</u> (major)

(4.53)   It's become very \<u>cold</u> | all of a /<u>sudden</u> (major + minor)

(4.54)   It's suddenly become very /<u>cold</u> ... (incomplete)

(4.55)   All of a /<u>sudden</u> | it's become very v<u>cold</u> (incomplete + implication)

(4.56)   All of a v<u>sudden</u> | it's become very \<u>cold</u> (theme highlighted + major)

4. Tones and the communicative functions

The tone system is used in English not only for the indication of information status but for another purpose, the indication of communicative functions. By 'communicative function' we mean the purpose for a given utterance intended by the speaker. For instance, is the speaker telling me something or asking me? Are they commanding me or requesting me to do something? The tone system is a guide, in a general sense, to such communicative functions.

The traditional view[9] is that statements – to sound like real statements – are accompanied by a falling tone, but genuine questions requiring an answer of either yes or no are accompanied by a rising tone. Commands have a fall, so do interjections, but question tags have either a fall or a rise depending on the speaker's sense of certainty or uncertainty. Questions with so-called *wh*-items are usually accompanied by a fall, too. This traditional view is largely borne out by extensive intonation analysis, but it only scratches the surface.

Before we begin a detailed discussion, we will consider briefly a question that must have come to mind. If the tone system of English realizes two quite different functions in spoken discourse, how can you tell when a rise, for instance, is indicating information status and when it is indicating a communicative function? The phonetic answer is easy in theory, but sometimes difficult in practice: a rise is operating in its informational capacity when it belongs to an intonation unit that is dependent upon another. When indicating either incomplete or minor information, its intonation unit is tied very closely – often with no pause – to another unit; such a unit acts as a kind of satellite to the other. The same is true of the non-final fall-rise indicating the highlighting of a theme; it is closely attached to another unit without pause. However, when a rise is operating in its communicative capacity, it is operating in an independent intonation unit, which is often separated from preceding and following units by a pause or even silence, or, of course, by a change of speaker. Furthermore, the rise for information status is usually confined to neutral rise, from low to mid; whereas the rise for communicative functions not only uses a neutral rise – and in that respect is wholly indistinguishable from its use in information status – it does have the potential for high and low variations to add an attitudinal dimension to the questions (or whatever).

In much informal conversation, with its false starts, hesitations, abandonments, etc., it is often difficult to apply the criteria of dependent and independent intonation units. For instance, when we considered a snippet of informal speech in Chapter 1 there was an intonation unit (1.3j) that was accompanied by a rise, but was preceded and followed by quite lengthy pauses. However, no one would interpret the unit *the gardens and houses but* as a question. But why not? For one thing, the whole discourse is marked by these quite lengthy pauses, which are the consequence of hesitation, looking for a word, thinking of what to say, etc. Secondly, the context does not suggest that a question is expected. And, thirdly, the grammatical structure of the words in the unit does not suggest that a question is intended. Where the phonetic clues are missing, semantic and syntactic clues help. It may well be that we rely on the semantic and syntactic clues more heavily than we do on the phonetic clues in interpreting a unit as a question; after all, we think we usually know when a question is being asked. It may well be the case that the phonetic clues provide confirmatory evidence rather than definitive evidence, especially in unrehearsed, spontaneous, informal speech.

From that discussion, you will notice that falling tones are associated not with satellite, dependent, units of intonation, but with the more central, nuclear, independent, units. This befits its designation of bearing major information. This particular status of the fall is bolstered by the observation that usually between half and two-thirds of all tones are falls. (We noted in Chapter 1 that prepared or rehearsed discourse has a relatively high proportion of rises, which demonstrates the planning of incomplete information with complete, but even so, half the tones are falls; the higher proportion of falls is found in unprepared, unrehearsed speech, up to 65 per cent.) Falls dominate, in both frequency and function, and this dominance is manifest in the tone system in communicative functions, too.

The dominance of the falling tone is manifest in two ways: first of all, even for the brief introduction to communicative functions given so far, there are more functions that use the fall than use the rise.

Communicative functions:	with fall;	with rise
statements	√	
yes/no questions		√
wh-questions	√	
question tags	√	√
commands	√	
interjections	√	

Secondly, the fall is associated with the speaker knowing something, telling something, and in the case of interjections, expressing their own feelings: the speaker's knowledge, authority and feelings dominate. On the other hand, the rise is associated with the speaker not knowing and therefore having to ask. The difference in the use of falls and rises in question tags mirrors that distinction: a fall represents the speaker being pretty sure and the rise the speaker being unsure. Generally speaking, a fall represents dominance and a rise deference.

But, you may ask, what about those questions that begin with *wh*-words (*who, whose, whom, what, which, where, when, why, how*)? Surely, they are questions that indicate the speaker's lack of knowledge, but they are accompanied with falls – and falls are associated with knowledge. The answer is quite simple. In the case of the *wh*-questions it is only one part of the whole proposition that is unknown. For instance, if I ask (example 1.5 in Chapter 1)

(4.57)   What are you going to \do tonight

it presupposes that I know that you are going to do something tonight; there is only one part of the whole proposition that I do not know, but the rest I do know. If, on the other hand, I ask

(4.58)   Are you going to /do anything tonight

I am indicating that I do not know if the proposition (that you are going to do something tonight) is valid or not. In the *wh*-question, I know that you have a plan; in the *yes/no* question, I don't know.

Here is another example:

(4.59)   When do you elect the Student Union \President

If I ask the question in the form of (4.59), it shows that I know there is to be an opportunity to elect the Student Union President; the only thing I do not know is when – but I know that the basic underlying proposition is valid. But if I ask

(4.60)   Do you elect the Student Union /President

then it indicates that I do not know about the system of Student Union presidential elections; I do not know whether the basic, underlying, proposition is valid or not.

The fall in (4.57) and (4.59) indicates my knowing; the rise in (4.58) and (4.60) indicates my not knowing and furthermore my deference to the knowledge that I presume my interlocutor possesses. So, although it may at first seem that a falling tone in a *wh*-question counters the general principle, it does in fact confirm it.

A fall indicates the speaker's certainty or dominance in respect of knowledge, authority and feelings; a rise indicates the speaker's uncertainty or deference to the knowledge – and, as we shall see, the authority and the feelings – of the person addressed.

This explanation of *wh*-questions having a fall can even be illustrated in very common questions like

(4.61)   What's the \time

(4.62)   What's your \name

(4.63)   Where do you \live

(4.64)   How \are you

The fall in each of these questions represents the speaker's presupposition of the validity of an underlying proposition, even if it is so obvious that to question it sounds odd: the time must be something, you must have a name, you must live somewhere, you must be in some kind of condition, and in the case of (4.65):

(4.65)   Who \are you

you must be somebody!

Three points must be noted. The first is that we are, in fact, again handling a speaker's perception of the communicative function, whether that perception is, in our estimation, accurate or not. A speaker may act as knowing something, but in fact be quite mistaken, as in

(4.66)   Twenty per cent means a \quarter

The speaker might in fact lie, but still acts as the one who knows and tells. Similarly, a speaker can ask a question even when they know the answer, what we call a rhetorical question; but the speaker has still got to use the appropriate rising tone to make it sound like a question:

(4.67)   Is that the right way to /do it

The second point is that there is always more than one way to intone an utterance. What appears on the surface as a statement can be intoned as a question; (4.66) could also be intoned as follows:

(4.68)   Twenty per cent means a /quarter

meaning something like a genuine, but challenging, question: 'Is that what you really think?' And (4.67) could be intoned with a fall:

(4.69)   Is that the right way to \do it

meaning something like a genuine, but challenging, statement: 'I think that is the wrong way to do it.'

Probably every example that has been given so far is capable of being intoned differently. But there is at least a tendency for declarative clauses, *wh*-interrogative clauses, imperative clauses and interjections to be intoned with a fall to effect, respectively, statements, *wh*-questions, commands and expressions of personal feelings; and for polar interrogative clauses to be intoned with a rise to effect a *yes/no* question.

The third point is an extension to the second. Although there is an observable tendency for declarative clauses, etc., to be intoned in a particular way, it is equally observable that clause types and communicative functions do not always match – as in (4.68) and (4.69) above. The tone system, however, always indicates the communicative function, whatever the clause type may be. It would be quite wrong to suggest that declarative clauses are realized by falls; it is not the clause that is realized by a tone, it is the communicative function. (4.68) and (4.69) above illustrate this. We can also illustrate this with a consideration of the intonation to the following imperative clauses:

(4.70)   Stop \talking

(4.71)   Take that silly \look off your face

(4.72)   Have a cup of \tea

(4.73)   Stir \well

(4.74)   Have a nice /time

(4.75)   Say that a/gain (and I'll \hit you)

(4.70) and (4.71) would no doubt be regarded as commands, and the speaker's authority is expressed in the choice of the fall. (4.72) and (4.73) are also imperatives with a falling tone, even though they are not, strictly speaking, commands; (4.72) might be interpreted as a recommendation, (4.73) as an instruction, but in both cases, the speaker still considers him- or herself to be the dominant partner in the exchange. (4.74) would seem strange with a fall, because we know that we cannot command a person to have a nice time; such a result is outside the speaker's control; it is, in fact, a wish, and because it is the listener's feelings that are affected, not the speaker's own feelings, a rise is the more appropriate choice of tone. (4.75) is a threat; it is the opposite of a command, the speaker does not wish the listener to repeat what they have already said. The rise, in this case, might simply be an indication of incompleteness, because the substance of the threat is yet to come.

It might also be noted that not all commands are necessarily issued in imperative clauses, but they must be accompanied by a fall to indicate the speaker's authority, e.g.:

(4.76)   Thou shalt have no other gods be\fore me

(4.77)   All library books must be returned by \Friday

(4.78)   Silence in \court

(4.79)   A\way with you all

5. Dominance and deference in communicative functions

We have seen that the traditional description of the intonation of communicative functions associates falls with statements, *wh*-questions, commands and interjections – all displaying the speaker's dominance in respect to information, authority and the expression of personal feelings – and rises with *yes/no* questions – displaying the speaker's deference to the hearer's assumed knowledge.

There are, however, very many more communicative functions than those just listed. The traditional list is based on the types of clauses recognized by grammarians: declarative for statements, two types of interrogatives for two types of questions, imperatives for commands, and verbless for interjections. We have already made the point that there is, in fact, no one-to-one correspondence between clause type and communicative function, that declarative clauses can be used for questions, interrogatives for statements, and imperatives for wishes, etc., and the second point that tones realize the communicative functions rather than the clause types. We have also, on a number of occasions, hinted at another point: that there are many more communicative functions than those recognized in traditional grammars. We have made reference to wishes, requests, instructions, recommendations, acknowledgement of the listener's personal feelings, and other functions like greeting, bidding farewell, thanking, apologizing, congratulating, and so on – all things we use language for.

Now, there is no special tone for each separate communicative function; the resources of intonation are simply not sufficient for so many different functions. The tone system simply indicates the speaker's status *vis-à-vis* the hearer: either as dominant or deferent. All the communicative functions can be grouped into three kinds: relating to knowledge in respect to information, reality and belief; to authority in respect of influencing other people's action ('suasion'); and to social interaction. We will now consider each of these three groups of communicative functions and show how the tone system operates to indicate dominance and deference.[10]

5.1 Information, reality and belief

In the area of information, reality and belief, there is a little more to be said. A fall indicates the speaker's dominance (knowledge) and a rise their deference to the presumed superior knowledge of the addressee. This is best seen in pairs of contrasting intonations units, as in (4.66) and (4.68) and in (4.67) and (4.69). The case of tags illustrates the general principle well:

(4.80)　　He's finished with my \book | \hasn't he

which sounds as if the speaker is pretty sure of the fact, and

(4.81)　　He's finished with my \book | /hasn't he

which sounds as if the speaker is not so sure.

In a study[11] of the succession of communicative functions in an ordinary piece of spontaneous informal dialogue the following functions were noted with falling tones: **statements, answers, explanations, reports, agreement, acknowledgement, descriptions, suppositions, hypotheses, deductions.** They all presuppose the speaker's dominance in knowing and telling.

The functions with an accompanying rise were *yes/no* **questions, appeals,** and **requests,** which are all functions in which the speaker acknowledges knowledge, or authority, in the addressee.

Other communicative functions that display the speaker's knowledge, and therefore are accompanied by a fall, are **denials, affirmations** and, of course, **disagreement.** The expressions of **doubt** and **hope** are, like suppositions and hypotheses, expressions of belief rather than knowledge; in these cases, the speaker's dominance is realized in the observation that it is the speaker's doubts, hopes, suppositions, hypotheses, etc. that are expressed. Expressions of doubt, for example, are typically accompanied by a falling tone:

(4.82)　　I doubt if he would \come

(4.83)　　I wouldn't have \thought so

(4.84)　　I can't imagine he \would

It is sometimes argued that the fall-rise properly expresses doubt. But this is not the case. In (4.82), doubt is expressed lexically, and in (4.83) and (4.84), by other wordings. It is true that these three utterances could have had a fall-rise, but the fall-rise itself does not mean doubt – otherwise (4.82) would have to be considered as doubly doubting. The fall-rise simply means that an extra message, an implication, is in the mind of the speaker, e.g.:

(4.85)   I doubt if he would ∨<u>come</u>

(4.86)   I ∨<u>doubt</u> if he would come

If we knew, or invented, a context, we could speculate on possible implications: perhaps for (4.85), 'So we'd better select someone else as goal-keeper', and for (4.86), 'but, of course, I can't be sure'.

Similarly, it has been argued that the expression of **possibility** is indicated by a fall-rise. Again, this is not so. Possibility can be indicated lexically as in (4.87) or grammatically as in (4.88):

(4.87)   It's \<u>possible</u>

(4.88)   I \<u>might</u> be able to play

The expression of possibility is quite simply accompanied by a fall. As with doubt, a fall-rise merely indicates implication: thus

(4.89)   It's ∨<u>possible</u>

and

(4.90)   I ∨<u>might</u> be able to play

might imply 'but I can't be certain'.

But what difference would a rising tone make in these instances?

(4.91)   It's ∕<u>possible</u>

(4.92)   I ∕<u>might</u> be able to play

The communicative function is now quite different. Imagine that somebody presents the proposition that the Monster Raving Loony Party could win a local by-election, and your answer is (4.91). What you are doing is conceding to your addressee that the proposition might be valid; you are deferring to the possible validity of the addressee's statement. Or, in the case of (4.92), you are unexpectedly invited to participate in a football match as the goalkeeper in a week's time; you concede the possibility. A **concession** is a kind of deference to somebody else's proposition; as such, it is signalled by a rising tone.

Contradictions are also signalled by a rising tone. You may wish to contest somebody's claim that you forgot all about some arrangement, by saying

(4.93)   Oh no I ∕<u>didn't</u>

Contradictions are regularly accompanied by a rise; it seems to signal that the other person may have grounds for making an assumption, e.g., in this case, your non-appearance at the meeting, and you concede that.

An excellent example of contradiction is found in the traditional pantomime where at one point a character at the front of the stage makes a claim which the audience can see is mistaken. There is usually a 'baddy' at the back of the stage, and the audience, especially the children, are encouraged to contradict the first character's claims, in a form like

(4.94)   Oh yes there /<u>is</u>

or

(4.95)   Oh no he /<u>isn</u>'t

Challenges also regularly take a rising tone. In one sense, a challenge, like a contradiction, is a concession to the other person's statement of fact, but there is an element of enquiry about it, too: 'Are you sure of your facts?' In response to someone's statement that her grandfather is travelling to Timbuktu, you might respond:

(4.96)   Your grandfather's travelling to Timbuk/<u>tu</u>

Because a challenge, by its very nature, is a strong expression, it is often accompanied by a rise to a high level.

Concessions, contradictions and challenges all typically take a declarative clause structure, but because of the sense of deference inherent in these communicative functions, a rising tone is appropriate. Challenges can, in fact, take the form of any clause type, because, in essence, a speaker who challenges uses the wording of the original, and the rise indicates as much as anything else: 'Is that really what you meant to say?' If the original was 'Let's go to the beach', the challenging response might be

(4.97)   Go to the beach on a day like /<u>this</u>

The term **echo question** is often used when an interrogative clause is being challenged. If you are asked if you are going to meet somebody whom you happen to dislike, you might respond

(4.98)   Am I going to meet /<u>him</u>

with the meaning of 'Can you really be serious in asking me such a question?' *Wh*-echo questions are common, with the tonic on the *wh*-item itself:

(4.99)   /<u>What</u> did you say you're going to do

(4.100)   /<u>When</u> is he coming

which can either have the force of a challenge or be a genuine request for a repetition of something you mistook or misheard.

Rises, of course, are most typical of **enquiries**, elicitations for information on the validity of a proposition, which are usually structured as polar interrogatives:

(4.101)   Are you going a∕<u>way</u> for Christmas

But just as rises can accompany declarative clauses, falls can accompany polar interrogatives. There is a kind of question that a speaker can employ not so much to make an enquiry, rather to guide the listener to taking a course of action or agreeing to an idea.

(4.102)   Are you \<u>sat</u>isfied now

really means 'I think you should be ...', and

(4.103)   Can you pay me by \<u>cheque</u> please

really means 'That's what I want you to do'. These **conducive questions** are not genuine enquiries after information, but are opinions stated in disguise.

    Guesses often take the form of a polar interrogative, but take a falling tone:

(4.104)   Have you heard all this be \<u>fore</u>

If (4.104) had been accompanied with a rise, it would have been interpreted as a genuine question, but the choice of a fall indicates the speaker's guess that the other person has indeed heard all this before.

    Denials can follow the same pattern. We have seen above that a denial takes a falling tone, because the speaker is sure of the facts. Denials may appear in polar interrogative form as well as declarative, but the sense of enquiry of the polar interrogative is countered by the fall:

(4.105)   Have I ever let you \<u>down</u>

meaning, of course, 'I have never...'[12]

    Exclamations, as we noted in Chapter 1, often take the form of a negative polar interrogative, e.g. *Isn't it hot*. A frequently used expression of exclamation when looking at a young infant is

(4.106)   Isn't he like his \<u>mother</u>

The falling tone makes this utterance unmistakably an exclamation.

    Two other typical communicative functions that combine polar interrogatives and falling tones are prompts and lead-ins. A **prompt** takes the form of a question, but its real intention is to get someone to comment on a matter. This is a technique often used by people interviewing on radio and television; here is an example from Brown's (1977) broadcast data:

(4.107)   Do you be\<u>lieve</u> that prices can be cur\<u>tailed</u>

What the interviewer was doing was prompting the politician to express an opinion, i.e. 'I want you to tell me whether...'

    Lead-ins are similar. A preliminary utterance to telling a joke often takes this form:

(4.108)   Have you heard the joke about the two poli\<u>ticians</u>

What this really means is 'I'm going to tell you a joke about ...' Similarly, an utterance like

(4.109)   Do you know about Mr \Evans

said without giving you a chance to reply is in fact just another way of saying 'Let me tell you about ...'

There are three other types of 'questions' that regularly take a falling tone. The first is a **repeat question**, as in

(4.110)   A: Do you want a cup of /tea

           B: /Pardon

           A: Do you want a cup of \tea

The fall in the response to *Pardon* seems to suggest something like 'What I said was ...', which is, of course, a statement. A well-known elementary course book for teaching English as a foreign language actually began with such a dialogue (see Figure 4.1).

The second is an **alternative question**, as in

(4.111)   A: Do you speak /French

           B: \No

           A: Do you speak \German then

The fall in the second interrogative seems to suggest 'Well, I will try...' which is, of course, a statement. This is similar to a **list question**, as in

(4.112)   Do you speak /French | /German | or I\talian

where the rises seem to indicate incomplete items in a list, and the fall the final item (see p. 36).

Finally, there are **second-attempt questions**, as in

(4.113)   A: Are you /going

           B: I don't \know

           A: Do you \want to go

The fall in the second interrogative suggests that the questioner is stepping back in the pursuit of finding a basis to proceed, meaning something like 'Well, what I need to know is ...', which is, of course, a statement.

We have seen, then, that a falling tone indicates the speaker's knowledge and certainty in respect of information, reality and belief: they know, and tell. A rising tone, on the other hand, indicates a deference to the other person's presumed knowledge: they don't know, and ask; or they acknowledge some degree of validity about the other person's knowledge. In general terms, a fall indicates the speaker's dominance, a rise the speaker's deference.

Lesson 1

Excúse me!

Yés?

Ís this your hándbag?

Párdon?

Ís thís yóur hándbag?

Yés, it is.

Thánk you véry múch.

Figure 4.1

5.2   Suasion

In a similar way, a fall indicates dominance in the realm of suasion, i.e. influencing people's action; a fall indicates the speaker's authority. Whether there is justification for such authority, or not, is not the issue: the speaker can act as one with authority. A rise indicates deference to the other person's authority or decision. The difference between a **command** and a **request** illustrates this. A person can only command if they have the authority to do so – whether the authority is legal, moral, physical, etc. With a request, a person asks another to do something, leaving the other person the ultimate decision to act, or not.

Compare, for instance, the difference between

(4.114)   Turn the \radio off

and

(4.115)   Turn the /radio off

The second sounds much gentler, more polite. Indeed, a person who regards themselves as having authority, may nevertheless decide to project themselves as less authoritative by deliberately choosing to use a rising tone. In general terms, then, in the realm of suasion a rise indicates deference to the other person's authority and decision: they don't decide, and must ask.

We will now consider other communicative functions from this point of view. A parent exercising authority over a child might say:

(4.116)   Don't talk with your \mouth full

On the other hand, that parent could try to achieve the same result by a different tactic:

(4.117)   Don't talk with your /mouth full

A straight **prohibition** requires a fall: a **plea**, a rise.

What is the difference in tactics between (4.118) and (4.119)?

(4.118)   Come \on

(4.119)   Come /on

The first could be interpreted as a **demand**: 'this is what you have to do'; the second is an example of coaxing: 'I do wish you would ...' The first has a ring of authority about it; the speaker has decided what you should do, and tells you. The second has a ring of wishing or pleading: it may indeed be uttered with a degree of forcefulness, but the speaker is **coaxing** rather than demanding. Commands, prohibitions and demands suggest speaker-dominance: requests, pleas and coaxing suggest deference – but, tactfully deployed, may achieve the results desired by the speaker!

Advice and **recommendations** are usually accompanied by falls because they contain a degree of authority on the part of the speaker. **Suggestions**

and **invitations** take a rise for, by their very nature, they allow the other person the final decision. Let us consider some examples:

(4.120)   You should take a little \break

(4.121)   You could take a little /break

The combination of the fall with a clause containing *should* will certainly be interpreted as advice: 'That's what I think you should do.' The rise and *could* are more likely to be thought of as communicating a suggestion: 'That's one possibility you could consider doing. The whole idea of advice contains the element of respect for the authority a person has. Suggestions are alternative courses of action, from which the other person can select; a suggestion may also be a single course of action for the other person to consider: either way, it is the other person who is left with the decision.

Now, if I follow the advice of (4.120) or the suggestion of (4.121), I might possibly ask 'Well, what shall I do?' The reply might be (4.122), or possibly (4.123):

(4.122)   How about a cup of \coffee

(4.123)   How about a cup of /coffee

In this pair, the wording is parallel, but again the fall of (4.122) expresses a recommendation and the rise of (4.123) an invitation.

Recommendations and invitations follow the same pattern, with the speaker's dominance in the former reflected in an accompanying fall, and the speaker's deference to the other person's decision in the latter in a rise.

(4.124)   You ought to try this new \coffee

(4.125)   Would you like to try this new /coffee

(4.126)   Have a \go

(4.127)   Have a /go (= 'Would you like to ...?')

However, if the lexical verbs *suggest, invite, request, plead* are used, they are not accompanied with a rise:

(4.128)   I suggest a cup of \coffee

(4.129)   I would like to invite you for \dinner

(4.130)   We request the pleasure of your \company

(4.131)   I'm \pleading with you

Why do these take a fall, when, after all, they actually contain the verbs that refer to the communicative function? One answer might be their greater deal of formality, but whatever the degree of formality, that should not alter the basic type of communication that they are. A better answer is that these utterances are really **announcements** of a suggestion, an invitation, a request and a plea; announcements derive from a speaker's decision: 'This is what I'm going to do – I'm going to ...' And speaker's decisions are indicated by falls.

Promises take a fall; the speaker has decided on a course of action and seeks to guarantee it:

(4.132)   I'll let you know to\morrow

(4.133)   We promise you a quick re\ply

Threats take a fall, too; a threat has all the features of a promise, but with a negative effect on the person addressed:

(4.134)   (Say that a/gain) and I'll \hit you

(4.135)   Don't you \dare tell lies

Offers take a rise: the speaker offers a course of action, but allows the other person to decide:

(4.136)   Can I /help you in any way

(4.137)   Another cup of /coffee

Warnings also take a rise; although the speaker warns, it is the person warned who has to take the decision; the speaker recognizes this with the choice of the rising tone:

(4.138)   Look where you're /going

(4.139)   /Careful

Offers and warnings can be announced by using the lexical verbs *offer* and *warn*; and as announcements, they are likely to be indicated by falls:

(4.140)   We offer the best service in the \town

(4.141)   I'm \warning you

Appeals take a rise. Appeals are attempts by a speaker to get the other person to reconsider a course of action, e.g.:

(4.142)   (A: I'll have to throw this coffee a\way)
           B: You don't have to do /that

(4.143)   (A: But the coffee tastes \awful)
           B: It's not /so bad

But the intention of an appeal is often to get the other person to consider a course of action favourably; this kind of appeal often takes the form of *you see, you must understand*, e.g.:

(4.144)   You /see (I've \got to pay him today)

(4.145)   You must under/stand (we can't af\ford a holiday)

The appeal may be directed at the other person's general knowledge, or particular local knowledge, or knowledge of a particular word; this kind of appeal usually takes the form of *you know*, e.g.:

(4.146)   We wanted to go to – you /<u>know</u> | that little place in \|taly | that's
           inde\<u>pendent</u>

(4.147)   (A: I'm going to get the \<u>tickets</u>)
           B: The /<u>tickets</u>

           A: You /<u>know</u> | the tickets for the \<u>circus</u>

(4.148)   Then they wanted to – you /<u>know</u> what I mean | what they did to
           \<u>Nixon</u>

The use of the lexical verb *appeal*, however, as in the other cases above, suggests an announcement rather than an appeal; hence a falling tone:

(4.149)   I'm appealing to your common \<u>sense</u>

Thus, in general terms, communicative functions that display the speaker's dominance – authority, decision-taking, announcing – are accompanied by a fall; those that display the speaker's deference to the other's authority or their right to decision-taking take a rise.

5.3   Social exchanges

The third category of communicative functions is social exchanges. These kinds of communication do not involve either the provision or elicitation of information, nor are they primarily intended to influence other people's action; they are simply intended to establish and maintain relationships between people; for instance, greeting and bidding farewell, introductions, attracting attention, apologizing, sympathizing, wishing, thanking, and so on. Once again, some of these functions seem naturally to require a fall, others a rise, and yet others either. Let us take greetings and farewells as examples.

Farewells are typically accompanied by a rising tone, e.g.:

(4.150)   Good/<u>bye</u>

(4.151)   Cheeri/<u>o</u>

(4.152)   See you a/<u>gain</u>

However, if the parting is regarded as only temporary, a fall accompanies the farewell, as if a piece of information is being given, e.g.:

(4.153)   See you this \<u>evening</u>

Greetings take either a fall or a rise, e.g.:

(4.154)   Good \<u>morning</u>

(4.155)   Good /<u>morning</u>

What is the difference? By now, you should be expecting the fall to indicate something akin to dominance, and the rise to deference; but in social exchange, what can dominate, and what can you defer to? In general terms, the answer is feelings. Falls tend to focus attention on the speaker's feelings, whereas the social functions in which the other person's feelings, or attention, are in focus, are expressed by means of the rise. In farewells, we attend to the other person's feelings: we are thinking of them, rather than ourselves, when we bid them farewell. If you say *Goodbye* with a fall, you invoke a very different situation:

(4.156)   Good\bye

It sounds very much like a dismissal in which the speaker's feelings dominate. The speaker's feelings dominate even more provocatively in

(4.157)   Good \riddance

which will only take a fall – a rise in (4.157) would sound like mocking.

But what is the difference between (4.154) and (4.155)? A rise in a greeting seems to suggest an interest in the person(s) addressed; O'Connor and Arnold (1973: 66) describe it as 'bright' and 'friendly'. This is not meant to suggest that the fall is unfriendly or unconcerned with the person(s) addressed; all it means is that the greeting with a fall is a plain greeting, possibly a little formal: 'I am greeting you.' The rise seems to mean 'I am acknowledging you as I greet'.

The same difference can be detected in **thanking**. A fall means: 'I am thanking you':

(4.158)   \Thank you

A rise seems to mean 'I am acknowledging you as the one I thank':[13]

(4.159)   /Thank you

Greetings and thanking seem to take a fall as a neutral tone, but a rise to indicate an interest in the feelings of the addressee. Greetings on the phone, however, generally take a rise:[14]

(4.160)   Hell/o

The speaker seems to be acknowledging the initiative taken by the caller, and thus defers to the caller's attention.

Welcomes take a fall; the speaker's sense of welcome seems to dominate:

(4.161)   \Welcome

(4.162)   How nice to \see you

(4.163)   Come on \in

Good wishes take a rise; inevitably it is the feelings of the other person(s) that are uppermost in the speaker's mind:

(4.164)   Happy /birthday

(4.165)   Have a nice /time

(4.166)   I hope you /pass

(4.167)   Do your /best

(4.168)   Bon voy/age

(4.169)   Remember me to your /father

(4.170)   Give my love to the /children

Toasts and congratulations take a fall; they are announcements of the speaker's feelings about somebody else's success or happiness. Typical toasts are:

(4.171)   Good \health

(4.172)   To the bride and \groom

(4.173)   Here's to a wonderful old \lady

(4.174)   \Cheers

and congratulations:

(4.175)   Well \done

(4.176)   Congratulations on your en\gagement

(4.177)   I was delighted to \hear about it

(4.178)   May we congratulate you on your recent ap\pointment

Praise, appreciation, approval and disapproval are all accompanied by a falling tone: it is the speaker's feelings that dominate, e.g.:

(4.179)   That's \great

(4.180)   It's a \lovely thought

(4.181)   You shouldn't have gone to so much \trouble

Expressions of regret take a rising tone, as befits a situation in which the feelings of the other person(s) are in focus:

(4.182)   I'm ever so /sorry

Apologies also take a rise, as they are regrets over what the speaker has done:

(4.183)   I do beg your /pardon

(4.184)   We won't let that happen a/gain

Sympathy also takes a rise, as a kind of regret over what has happened to the other person(s):

(4.185)   That's a /pity

(4.186)   It's a great /shame

(4.187)   I was sorry to hear about your father's /<u>ac</u>cident

When regret is communicated via exclamations, however, the exclamation retains its falling tone:

(4.188)   What a \\<u>pity</u>

(4.189)   How \\<u>awful</u>

(4.190)   What a terrible \\<u>shock</u>

A **request for forgiveness** follows the normal pattern for requests, with a rise. And **granting** forgiveness or reassurance is also accompanied by a rise as the speaker acknowledges the other person's feelings:

(4.191)   That's all /<u>right</u>

(4.192)   It doesn't /<u>matter</u>

A **request for attention**, however, follows the normal pattern for implication; in addition to soliciting somebody's attention, there is a requirement of some service:

(4.193)   Exv<u>cuse</u> me

(4.194)   v<u>Waiter</u>

(4.195)   v<u>Nurse</u>

A vocative can also function as a request for attention:

(4.196)   Ev<u>lizabeth</u>

(4.197)   v<u>John</u>

An equivalent with a fall sounds more like a **summons**, in which a speaker's feelings or sense of authority dominate:

(4.198)   E\\<u>lizabeth</u>

(4.199)   \\<u>John</u>

(4.200)   \\<u>Waiter</u>

or even

(4.201)   Ex\\<u>cuse</u> me

With a rise, they sound like enquiries:

(4.202)   E/<u>lizabeth</u> ('Are you there?')

Introductions usually take the form of a request (with a rising tone) and an announcement (with a falling tone):

(4.203)   /<u>John</u> | I would like you to meet my \\<u>father-in-law</u>

(4.204)   Miss /<u>Jones</u> | this is Mr \\<u>Evans</u>

And finally, indicating different kinds of attention is also a function of the tone system. This is often referred to as **back channel**; it is the means by which one person indicates a degree of attention to what another is saying. Back channel takes the form of signals like *yes, no, oh, mm,* spoken quietly and usually with a fairly narrow range of pitch. A falling tone indicates agreement and a rising tone a wish for the current speaker to continue:

(4.205) ˎm

(4.206) ˏm

An alternative to the rise, a mid-level pitched tone may simply mean 'I am still listening':

(4.207) –m

5.4 Conclusion

In the second half of this chapter, we have seen, from many examples, that in addition to the role of expressing the speaker's choice in respect of status of information the tone system has a role in expressing the speaker's choice of type of interaction with the addressee. It is a simple system that covers a wide range of communicative functions; it covers, in fact, all types of communicative functions: a fall indicates the speaker's dominance in knowing and telling something, in telling someone what to do, and in expressing their own feelings; a rise indicates the speaker's deference to the addressee's knowledge, their right to decide, and their feelings. Calls for attention require fall-rises because a need for service is implied; otherwise calls with falls indicate a summons for attention (speaker's dominance), and with rises they indicate enquiries (speaker's deference).

Notes

1. The inadequacy of punctuation symbols to represent intonation is amply illustrated in the work of many conversational analysts.
2. Palmer (1922) and Halliday (1967) both suggest that the high rise is a primary tone in contrast with the low rise (described here as neutral). Most others do not make such a distinction: see Tench (1990: 448–54) for a full discussion.
3. Halliday's scheme, together with Ladd's (1980) exposition, are extensively discussed in Tench (1990: 219–38).
4. This widespread agreement is shared by Armstrong and Ward (1931: 22), Pike (1945: 51–9), Kingdon (1958: 73, 221: 'prelusory'), Crystal (1975: 35: 'non-final tonic'), O'Connor and Arnold (1973: 88–9: 'non-final'), Brazil et al. (1980: 86–90), Cruttenden (1986: 102–3), as well as Halliday (1967, 1970).
5. See Halliday (1970: 62–3) for further examples, and also Brazil et al. (1980: 86–90, for the 'oblique' tone), Crystal (1975: 34–5) and Cruttenden (1986: 102–3).
6. See Halliday (1967: 45) for a similar case.
7. See Halliday (1985: 56–9) for the explication of clauses as themes.

8. See Palmer (1922), Armstrong and Ward (1931), Pike (1945: 50), Kingdon (1958: 29-30), O'Connor and Arnold (1973: 68-9: 'contrast', 'concession'), Crystal (1975: 36). Ladd has a long and valuable discussion (1980: 145-62).

9. See O'Connor and Arnold (1973), Gimson (1989), Thompson (1981), Baker (1982), Hooke and Rowell (1982).

10. I am indebted to Leech and Svartvik (1994) for this threefold categorization of communicative functions.

11. Tench (1990: 318-33).

12. See Hudson (1975) for a further discussion of these points.

13. See Knowles (1989: 195) for a similar treatment.

14. This was noted as early as 1945 by Pike (1945: 68); see also Leech and Svartvik (1994: para. 358).

5

Tone variations

1. Attitudinal meanings

We now come to that part of the intonation system that is most familiar to everyone, but it has been necessary to show how this part actually belongs to a much broader set of systems. We have already referred on a number of occasions to that familiar observation about it not being what someone said that concerned us but the way they said it. 'The way they said it' actually usually refers to the kind of attitude that is detected in the speaker's voice, whether the speaker was angry, or civil, or grumbling, or enthusiastic, and so on. This attitudinal function, as has been frequently pointed out, is only one of the kinds of meaning that intonation is used to express, but it is the kind of meaning that most people are most aware of.

We have seen that intonation is used for managing the organization of information – units, focus, status – and, incidentally, for distinguishing between various syntactic possibilities; people are less aware of these functions because they are part of the ideational content of the message. (In the same way, people are not so aware of grammatical constructions and lexical choices – we do not, as a rule, think about them; we just use them.) People are, possibly, more aware of intonation's use in communicative functions, because they have to respond to them in an appropriate way, but people are most aware of the attitudinal function of intonation, because it tells them something about the person who is speaking.

What are the kinds of variations to the tones that are used for attitudinal purposes? There are variations to the degree of falling, rising and falling-rising, either greater or lesser than the neutral forms, and there are variations in the pitch movements in the pre-tonic segment, i.e. the head and the pre-head. The two kinds of variations are called, as we noted in the previous chapter, **secondary tones**, and the role they play can be described as follows: once a person has decided to communicate in speech (rather than writing) and has formulated a message (in terms of lexis and grammar), that person then has to encode that message phonologically in terms of

1   the consonants, vowels and stress patterns of the words
2   the rhythm and intonation of the syntax of the clauses
3   the units, focus and status of the successive pieces of information
4   communicative functions
5   and, if desired, by means of the secondary tones, an indication of a state of mind.

There are, in fact, other considerations also, and a fuller picture will be presented in the next chapter, but at this juncture it should be noted that the expression of attitude is an optional element, whereas all the other elements are essential to the communication of any spoken message. Attitudinal expression is described here as optional simply because there are modes of presentation in which it is not generally included; in newsreading, for instance, it is kept to a minimum; in unison prayer, it is impossible. In informal, spontaneous conversation, attitudes are expressed, but not necessarily all the time; there will be periods of time in a conversation when speakers are merely telling, or reporting, but there will be other periods when they add their feelings to the messages. Notice that feelings are **added** to items that are already, and necessarily, there: the ideational, interactional and textual components are obligatory, the attitudinal component is optional.

Linguists have not always thought of intonation's role in expressing attitude as being additional. Indeed, many of the best-known descriptions of English intonation of the past have regarded the attitudinal function as primary and central: Pike (1945), Crystal (1969), O'Connor and Arnold (1973). This is but a reflection of people's greater general awareness of that function than of the other functions. Other descriptions have placed the organization of information and discourse functions as central, but have nevertheless acknowledged the additional expression of attitude: Halliday (1967), Brown (1977), Brazil et al. (1980), Ladd (1980); and Crystal (1975) also now follows this line. All are nevertheless agreed that intonation is a means by which attitude is expressed in speech.

2. Intonational lexicons

What kinds of attitudes get expressed? This is not an easy question to answer, and the inconsistencies between one description and another (and indeed even within descriptions) are testimony to this difficulty. A novel suggestion was made by Liberman (1979) that there is a kind of **lexicon** of intonational meanings. What he meant was that just as you can make a list of words, you can make a list of intonation patterns, with each pattern having a particular meaning; furthermore, just as words are composed of morphemes, intonation patterns consist of morpheme-like components (pitch movements in the head and the tonic) which can be assembled in different ways to represent different meanings. Ladd (1980) followed up the same idea and suggested that these intonational lexicons covered not only expressions of attitude but other kinds of meaning, too. However, the idea has been mainly confined to the attitudinal function, and that is how we shall consider the notion of an intonational lexicon in this chapter.

The descriptions of English intonation listed above can all be presented as intonational lexicons. We shall begin with an outline of O'Connor and Arnold's (1973) description, because it is perhaps the most famous in the English language classrooms of the world and because it attempts to be fully comprehensive. Liberman himself commented that their description was the 'nearest thing available to an adequate intonational lexicon' (Liberman, 1979: 94).

2.1 O'Connor and Arnold

Their description is set out in Table 5.1 on pp. 113–15. We will illustrate each of the ten patterns with an example from their own drills. Pattern 1, which they call the 'low drop', has, in its fullest form, a low pre-head, a high head and a low fall:

(5.1)   (A: Have you any news of /Malcolm)
        B: He's passed his e\xam

The pre-head *He's* is low, there is a jump up at the onset syllable of the head, *passed*; the pitch remains relatively high for *his* and *e-*; there is a small jump down to about mid, or low-mid pitch for the tonic, which is then itself accompanied by a short fall to a low pitch.[1] The meaning of this pattern is given as 'categoric, weighty, judicial, considered'.

Pattern 2, the 'high drop':

(5.2)   (A: Where on earth are my \slippers)
        B: I can't think \what's happened to them

The pattern of pre-head and head is the same as for pattern 1; the only difference is that the fall in the tonic begins from the high pitch level of the head and finishes at a low pitch. The meaning of this higher pitched fall is given as 'conveying a sense of involvement, light, airy'.

Pattern 3, the 'take off':

(5.3)   (A: Let me get you some more \tea)
        B: You're very /kind

The pre-head (*you're*) and head (*very*) are kept low and the rise in the tonic is a low rise. Its meaning is given as 'encouraging further conversation, guarded, reserving judgement, appealing to the listener to change his (*sic*) mind, deprecatory, (in contradictions) resentful'.

Pattern 4: the 'low bounce':

(5.4)   (A: I \hate | climbing /ladders)
          B: It's all /right

The pre-head (*It's*) is low, the head (*all*) is high; the voice then jumps down to low in order to effect a low rise in the tonic. Its meaning is given as 'soothing, reassuring, hint of great self confidence and self-reliance; (in echoes) questioning with a tone of surprise and disbelief; (in non-final word groups) creating expectancy about what is to follow'.

Pattern 5, the 'switchback':

(5.5)   (A: Do you /smoke)
          B: I do ∨sometimes

The pre-head (*I*) is low; the voice then jumps up to a high level on the onset syllable of the head (*do*) and then falls during the production of the head – in this case, it is only the single syllable, *do*; finally, the voice jumps back up to high in order to effect the fall-rise in the tonic: the fall accompanies the tonic syllable itself, *some-* and the rise is left to the final syllable, *-times*. Its meaning is given as 'grudgingly admitting, reluctantly or defensively dissenting, concerned, reproachful, hurt, reserved, tentatively suggesting: (in echoes) greatly astonished'.

Pattern 6, the 'long jump':

(5.6)   (A: ∨Mary likes it)
          B: Yes but I \don't

Again the pre-head is low (*Yes but*), the head (*I*) rises, and the tonic falls. Its meaning is given as 'protesting, as if suffering under a sense of injustice'.

Pattern 7, the 'high bounce':

(5.7)   (A: Alan's not \here I'm afraid)
          B: He's gone /home

The pre-head (*He's*) is low; the voice jumps to high on the onset syllable of the head and remains high through the head (*gone*); the voice then jumps down to low or mid-low in order to effect a high rise in the tonic. Its meaning is given as 'questioning, trying to elicit a repetition, but lacking any suggestion of disapproval or puzzlement; (in non-final word groups) casual, tentative'.

Pattern 8, the 'jackknife':

(5.8)   (A: Did you /like it)
          B: I simply ∧hated it

The pre-head (*I*) is low; the voice jumps to high on the onset syllable of the head and remains high for the remainder of the head (*simply*); then it jumps down to mid or mid-low in order to effect a rise-fall, the rise accompanying the tonic syllable, *ha-*, and the fall the tail, *-ted it*. Its meaning is given as 'impressed, awed, complacent, self-satisfied, challenging, censorious, disclaiming responsibility'.

Pattern 9, the 'high dive':

(5.9)   (A: Which are \our places)
          B: `There's | ⁄yours

This ninth pattern is actually a sequence of patterns 2 and 3, which we would interpret as a sequence of two intonation units. O'Connor and Arnold treat it as a single pattern and give its meaning as 'appealing to the listener to continue with the topic of conversation; expressing gladness, regret, surprise'.

Pattern 10, the 'terrace':

(5.10)   (A: What re\action did you get)
          B: John and –George | seemed rather `keen

Pattern 10 has a low pre-head (not realized in the above example), a high head (*John and*) and then a mid-level pitch on the tonic (*George*); then it must be followed by another intonation unit. The meaning of pattern 10 is given as 'marking non-finality without conveying any expression of expectancy'.

The reasons for taking the trouble to exemplify all ten patterns are twofold: first, to demonstrate some of the pitch variations involved in the pre-tonic and the tonic; and second, to illustrate some of the attitudes that get expressed by intonation.

The pitch variations, demonstrated above, include low, high, falling, and rising heads, and high, low and rising-falling variations to the tones. The pre-head was uniformly low in all ten patterns: however, O'Connor and Arnold's system of description includes a supplementary set of ten patterns, all with high pre-head, with the general meaning of 'emphatic'. The 'emphatic' set also involves three other types of head: stepping, sliding and climbing heads.

The stepping head has a high onset, but each stressed syllable in the remainder of the head steps down slightly in pitch:

(5.11)   I 'simply 'don't know 'what to \do

The onset syllable is *sim-* and the remaining stressed syllables in the head are *don't* and *what*, each on a slightly lower pitch than that of the preceding stressed syllable. Its meaning is simply given as 'emphatic'.

The sliding head has a high onset but it 'slides' to a lower pitch; each succeeding stressed syllable in the head also begins relatively high and slides down, producing a series of falls before the main fall in the tonic. The climbing head is the reverse, with a series of rises in the head, before the fall in the tonic. These two variations to the pitch pattern of the head are said to reinforce the sense of emphasis.

(5.12)   I \simply \don't know \what to \<u>do</u>

(5.13)   I /simply /don't know /what to \<u>do</u>

Thus O'Connor and Arnold have an intonational lexicon of twenty patterns, with a range of meanings each. Two points can be made about the range they present. The first is that in fact it is more complicated than it appears above, because for all the patterns, different ranges of meanings can be ascribed to statements, *wh*-questions, *yes/no* questions, commands and interjections.[2] The meanings illustrated in the above thirteen examples all relate to statements; different ranges of meanings are ascribed to the other clause types.

The second point is that the range of meanings seems so wide, indeed too wide to possess any general sense. You may indeed have wondered whether some of the meanings were really appropriate. For instance, is the reply in (5.3) above intended to encourage further conversation? Not necessarily, since it might simply be a polite acknowledgement of the other person's offer, and no more. Is the reply in (5.3) above guarded? This meaning seems wholly inappropriate. Nor does it appear as intended to reserve judgement to appeal to the listener to change his (*sic*) mind! It certainly isn't deprecatory, nor does it convey a resentful contradiction. It is, as mentioned above, nothing other than a simple, but polite, acknowledgement of the other person's offer (see Chapter 4).

The problem with O'Connor and Arnold's meanings is that they are as diverse as the types of situations they had in mind. Very often it is not the intonation pattern that has suggested a particular meaning, but the choice of lexis and the situation itself in which the utterances are made. That is why the range of meanings for (5.3) above is so wide and diverse. Check through the ranges of meanings for the other patterns; look, for instance, at the range credited to the eighth pattern: can you think of different situations in which any of the suggested meanings would be appropriate, and different words, too? A learner of the language may well be bemused by the indication of the meaning of pattern 8 as either impressed or complacent or challenging or censorious, and so on; how does the learner know which of these varied ascriptions is being meant by any given instance of pattern 8? The truth is that those ascriptions rely on the choice of lexis and a particular situation, whereas the real meaning of the intonation pattern is something else.

TABLE 5.1 O'Connor and Arnold's (1973) system of Intonation

---

1. Low drop. (a) no head, low fall
                (b) low pre-head – high head – low fall

Attitude

In STATEMENTS: with no head, detached, cool, dispassionate, reserved, dull, possibly grim or surly; with a high head, categoric, weighty, judicial, considered.

In *WH*-QUESTIONS: with no head, detached, flat, unsympathetic, even hostile; with a high head, searching, serious, intense, urgent.

In *YES/NO* QUESTIONS: with no head (in tags used as independent comments), uninterested, hostile; with a high head, serious, urgent.

In COMMANDS: with no head, unemotional, calm, controlled, cold; with a high head, very serious, very strong.

In INTERJECTIONS: with no head, calm, unsurprised, reserved, self-possessed; with a high head, very strong.

---

2. High drop: low pre-head – high head – high fall

Attitude

In STATEMENTS: conveying a sense of involvement, light, airy.

In *WH*-QUESTIONS: brisk, businesslike, considerate, not unfriendly, lively, interested.

In *YES/NO* QUESTIONS: willing to discuss but not urgently, sometimes sceptical; (in question tags used as independent comments) mildly surprised acceptance of the listener's premises.

In COMMANDS: suggesting a course of action and not worrying about being obeyed.

In INTERJECTIONS: mildly surprised, not so reserved or self-possessed as with the low drop.

---

3. Take off: low pre-head – low head – low rise

Attitude

In STATEMENTS: encouraging further conversation, guarded, reserving judgement, appealing to the listener to change his mind, deprecatory, (in contradictions) resentful; in non-final word groups, deprecatory.

In *WH*-QUESTIONS: with the nuclear tone on the interrogative word, wondering, mildly puzzled; otherwise, very calm, but very disapproving and resentful.

In *YES/NO* QUESTIONS: disapproving, sceptical.

In COMMANDS: (beginning with *Don't*) appealing to the listener to change his mind; (in a few short commands) calmly warning, exhortative.

In INTERJECTIONS: sometimes reserving judgement, sometimes calm, casual acknowledgement.

113

4. Low bounce: (a) low pre-head – high head – low rise
(b) high pre-head – low rise

Attitude

In STATEMENTS: soothing, reassuring, hint of great self-confidence and self-reliance; (in echoes) questioning with a tone of surprise and disbelief; (in non-final word groups) creating expectancy about what is to follow.

In WH-QUESTIONS: with the nuclear tone on the interrogative word, puzzled; (in echoes) disapproving; otherwise, sympathetically interested.

In YES/NO QUESTIONS: genuinely interested.

In COMMANDS: soothing, encouraging, calmly patronizing.

In INTERJECTIONS: airy, casual yet encouraging, often friendly, brighter than when said with the take off.

---

5. Switchback: low pre-head – falling head – fall-rise

Attitude

In STATEMENTS: grudgingly admitting, reluctantly or defensively dissenting, concerned, reproachful, hurt, reserved, tentatively suggesting; (in echoes) greatly astonished.

In QUESTIONS: (in echoes) greatly astonished; otherwise, interested and concerned as well as surprised.

In COMMANDS: urgently warning with a note of reproach or concern.

In INTERJECTIONS: scornful.

---

6. Long jump: low pre-head – rising head – high fall

Attitude

In STATEMENTS: protesting, as if suffering under a sense of injustice.

In WH-QUESTIONS: protesting, somewhat unpleasantly surprised.

In YES/NO QUESTIONS: willing to discuss but protesting the need for settling a crucial point.

In COMMANDS: recommending a course of action but with a note of critical surprise.

In INTERJECTIONS: protesting, surprised.

---

7. High bounce: low pre-head – high head – high rise

Attitude

In STATEMENTS: questioning, trying to elicit a repetition, but lacking any suggestion of disapproval or puzzlement; (in non-final word groups) casual, tentative.

In WH-QUESTIONS: with the nuclear tone on the interrogative word, calling for a repetition of the information already given; with the nuclear tone following the interrogative word, either echoing the listener's question before going on to answer it or (in straightforward, non-echo questions) tentative, casual.

In YES/NO QUESTIONS: either echoing the listener's question or (in straightforward, non-echo questions) light and casual.

In COMMANDS and INTERJECTIONS: querying all or part of the listener's command or interjection, but with no critical intention.

> 8.   Jackknife: low pre-head – high head – rise-fall
>
> Attitude
>
> In STATEMENTS: impressed, awed, complacent, self-satisfied, challenging, censorious, disclaiming responsibility.
>
> In *WH-*QUESTIONS: challenging, antagonistic, disclaiming responsibility.
>
> In *YES/NO* QUESTIONS: impressed, challenging, antagonistic.
>
> In COMMANDS: disclaiming responsibility, sometimes hostile.
>
> In INTERJECTIONS: impressed, sometimes a hint of accusation.

> 9.   High dive = High drop (2) + Take off (3)
>
> Attitude
>
> In STATEMENTS: appealing to the listener to continue with the topic of conversation; expressing gladness, regret, surprise.
>
> In QUESTIONS: very emotive, expressing plaintiveness, despair gushing warmth.
>
> In COMMANDS: pleading, persuading.
>
> In INTERJECTIONS: intensely encouraging, protesting.

> 10.   Terrace: low pre-head – high head – mid-level
>
> Attitude
>
> In ALL sentence types: (in non-final word groups) marking non-finality without conveying any impression of expectancy.
>
> In STATEMENTS AND INTERJECTIONS: (in final word groups) calling out to someone as from a distance.

2.2   Pike

We turn now to Pike (1945). Despite recent interest in American intonation, Pike's description remains the only comprehensive attempt, and has been admired as such by generations of American teachers of English. Crystal described it as the 'first really thorough description of the intonation system of any dialect of English' (Crystal, 1969: 47) and Cruttenden concedes that it has not been surpassed in America for comprehensiveness (Cruttenden, 1986: xi).

His orientation, like O'Connor and Arnold's, was the attitudinal function. He said as much in these two quotations:

> In English, then, an INTONATION MEANING modifies the lexical meaning of a sentence by adding to it the SPEAKER'S ATTITUDE toward the contents of that sentence (or an indication of the attitude with which the speaker expects the hearer to react).   (Pike, 1945: 21)

and:

Contour (= tone)	Descriptive label	Excessive use
falls	'contrastive pointing'	
falls to low (4)	finality	
2–4	S: moderate, contrastive pointing *Wh*: most frequent *Y/N*: insistent	
1–4	intense + unexpected + contrastive pointing	gushiness
? 4	mild + detached + contrastive pointing	professional aloofness
3–4 'with creak'	mild unpleasantness	grouchiness
falls to mid-low (3)	non-finality, less prominence	
2–3	mild, 'very frequent and normal' endearment (with female speakers)	
1–3	intense + unexpected	
falls to mid-high (2)	light ('endearing	baby talk
1–2	encouragement', etc.)	
rises	incomplete, needing supplementation (from speaker/hearer); polite, cheerful	
rises from mid-low (3)		
3–2	S: incomplete sequence *Y/N:* question	
3–1	incomplete sequence + intense + unexpected/polite	
rises from low (4)		
4–3	incomplete, needing supplementation + deliberative	
4–2	incomplete, needing supplementation + deliberative + sequence	deliberate hearty cheerfulness
4–1	incomplete, needing supplementation, deliberative + intense	
rises from mid-high (2)	incomplete sequence +	insincere politeness
2–1	mild, polite	unctuous manner

TABLE 5.2 Pike's (1945) lexicon (S = statement; *Wh* = *wh*-question; *Y/N* = *yes/no* question)

fall-rises

rising from 3 to 2

2-3-2	implication, non-finality
1-3-2	implication, non-finality + intense/unexpected

rising from 4 to 3

2-4-3	implication, incomplete + deliberative
1-4-3	implication, incomplete + deliberative + intense/unexpected
3-4-3	implication, incomplete sequence + deliberative + mild/detached

rising from 4 to 2

2-4-2	implication, incomplete sequence + deliberative
1-4-2	implication, incomplete sequence + deliberative + intense/unexpected

rising from 4 to 1

2-4-1	implication, incomplete sequence + deliberative + unexpected/polite
1-4-1	implication, incomplete sequence + deliberative + intense

rise-falls

4-3-4	repudiation

complex

2-4 + 3-3	mildly poignant
3-1 + 4-3	encouragement
precontour 2 + 4-4	suspended conclusion

level (in final position)

	strong implication (without further differentiation)
2-2	
3-3	
4-4	

> For English, meanings of English intonation contours are largely of [this] general type – ATTITUDES of the speaker (or, occasionally, imputed by the speaker to the hearer). Most sentences or parts of sentences can be pronounced with several different intonation contours, according to the speaker's momentary feeling about the subject matter. These attitudes can vary from surprise, to deliberation, to sharp isolation of some part of a sentence for attention, to mild intellectual detachment.   (ibid.: 23)

Pike's description of American intonation rests on an analysis of four pitch levels (not five, as used in Chapter 4), with falls, rises, fall-rises and rise-falls beginning and ending on one particular pitch. Pitch level 1 corresponds to high, and thus a 1–4 fall would be a fall from high to low; pitch level 2 corresponds to mid/mid-high, and thus a 2–4 fall would correspond to the kind of fall that we have described as neutral; pitch level 3 corresponds to mid-low/mid, and thus a 3–4 fall would correspond to a low fall. Falls can also drop to only level 3, or even level 2.[3] Rises have a corresponding range of starting and ending points. The full description appears in summary form in Table 5.2; it consists of a lexicon of 29 patterns (or 'contours' as he preferred to call them), including three complex patterns.

What is immediately apparent in a comparison with O'Connor and Arnold is that whereas Pike's description is as comprehensive – in fact, it includes more patterns – its meaning labels are much less diffuse and in most cases not specified to particular clause types. What Pike had done was find a much more uniform, and simpler, system of attitude ascriptions.

However, the question arises about the nature of some of the ascriptions. In what sense can 'incomplete sequence' or 'question' be called an attitude? The same criticism could legitimately be levelled against O'Connor and Arnold at times, e.g. for pattern 10, the label 'marking non-finality without conveying any expression of expectancy' is hardly an attitude. What Pike and, later, O'Connor and Arnold realized is that intonation performs, in fact, more than one function, but they never reached the systematic exposition of the variety of functions as featured in this present description of intonation.

Not only is Pike's description more systematic than O'Connor and Arnold's, but it is also possible to display a kind of morphology of meanings. It is possible to isolate individual meanings of most levels and movements and thereby establish basic elements of intonation, 'somewhat analogous to morphemes, which may combine to form words' (Liberman, 1979: 133). Pike did not, in fact, display such a 'tonal morphology', but it can be abstracted from the general description, and it must have existed in his mind as an operating system, to produce the kind of consistency that appears in his work. The abstracted 'tonal morphology' appears in Table 5.3.

A Contours

falls to 4	\4	finality	falls from 2	2\	moderate
falls to 3	\3	non-finality	one level falls	\1\	mild
falls to 2	\2	lightness	falls from 1	1\	intense/ unexpected
rises from 3	3/	incomplete	rises to 3	/3	incomplete
rises from 4	4/	deliberative	rises to 2	/2	sequences
rises from 2	2/	polite	rises to 1	/1	intense (except 2–1 = polite)
fall-rises	∨	implication			
(low) rise-fall	∧	repudiation			
levels (in final position)	–	strong implication			
2–4 + 3–3	\+–	mild poignancy			
3–1 ı 4–3	/+,	encouragement			
precontour 2 + 4–4	–_	suspended conclusion			

B Precontours

level	3		neutral
	2		insistent
	1		insistent + unexpected
	4		highlighting of focus
slurred		↗	protesting
		↘	insistent
descending stress		– – _	intense precision
deferred		＼u＼u＼u	(long precontour)

TABLE 5.3 Pike's (1945) tonal morphology

2.3 Halliday and 'key'

Halliday (1967, 1970) attempted to combine attitudinal meanings into one general intonation system, which also included information structure, syntactic contrasts and the communicative functions. The part of the general system that 'controlled' attitudinal meanings he called 'key', and 'key' was principally realized in the secondary tones. (It was Halliday who provided the concept of primary and secondary tones.)

Unlike the description of English tones presented in Chapter 4, Halliday proposed five primary tones: 1 (fall), 2 (high rise), 3 (low rise), 4 (fall-rise) and 5 (rise-fall). The rise-fall is typically used for strong assertions; and, in our view, the high rise indicates a strength of feeling in challenging a statement or in seeking information. The pre-tonic variations of pitch which Halliday included in his description are rising, falling, level (high, mid and low), uneven

Pre-tonic	Tone	Tone number	Descriptive label
mid, even	fall	1	S,C,*Wh*,Ex: neutral *Y/N*: strong (forceful or impatient)
rising	high fall	1+	strong or unexpected
falling	low fall	1−	mild or expected
glissando rising	fall	−1	forceful or querulous
high/falling	high rise	2	S, Ex: statement-question, seeking confirmation; contradiction, denial or disappointing of expectation *Wh*: mild (tentative or deferential) *Y/N*: neutral
high/falling	high fall – high rise	<u>2</u>	*Y/N*: specifying the particular point of the query
low	high rise	−2	*Y/N*: intense, showing surprise (incl. disapproval), concern
(mid, even)	low rise	3	S: acceding to request, unexpressed expectation; reassurance C: mild, request; polite (with negative C)
low	low rise	3	expressing unconcern, uncertainty
falling to mid	fall-rise	4	S: reservation,contrast, personal opinion offered for consideration
glissando falling	low fall-rise	<u>4</u>	S: exclusive, contrastive, strong reservation
rising	rise-fall	5	S: asserting, expressing some other form of commitment, surprise, personal reaction (favourable or unfavourable)
glissando rising	low rise-fall	<u>5</u>	S: intense, showing awe (which may be sarcastic) or disappointment

TABLE 5.4 Halliday's 1967/1970 lexicon
(S = statement; C = command; *Wh* = *wh*-question; *Y/N* = *yes/no* question; Ex = exclamation)

(= O'Connor and Arnold's 'climbing head') and listing (a series of low rises before the tonic, each low rise indicating one listed term). Halliday proposed a lexicon of fourteen patterns, as displayed in Table 5.4.

Halliday's labels are as pithy and systematic as Pike's, but he distinguishes less than half the number of patterns. Halliday also has a system of neutral tones for certain clause types: for example, whereas a fall is neutral for statements, commands, *wh*-questions and exclamations, it is not neutral for *yes/no* questions: a fall with a *yes/no* question is said to indicate 'forcefulness' or 'impatience'. In this case, 'key' is actually realized as a basic tone, but in combination with a clause type in which it is not neutral.

2.4 Crystal

Crystal (1969) investigated the expression of attitude by asking people to perform a set of sentences in a way that expressed a particular attitude. The twenty attitudes that Crystal selected were: *haughty, puzzled, amused, pleased, questioning, worried, dismayed, disapproving, vexed, conspiratorial, impatient, satisfied, grim, excited, precise, angry, matter-of-fact, bored, irritated, apologetic.* Ignoring, for our present purpose, matters of tonality and tonicity, we note the following prosodic and paralinguistic features required for Crystal's system for the expression of attitudinal meaning by intonation:

> nuclear tone type
>
> strong stressed syllables
>
> high unstressed syllables
>
> clipped syllables
>
> drawled syllables
>
> simple pitch range (syllabic): large step-up, slight/no step-up, step-down
>
> 'flattened' syllables in tail
>
> complex pitch range: narrow, wide
>
> simple pitch range over a polysyllabic stretch: high, low
>
> loudness: loud, soft
>
> tempo: fast, slow
>
> rhythmicality
>
> tension: tense, lax
>
> paralinguistic features

However, a very simple attitudinal lexicon appeared in Crystal (1975: 38), based on seven tones occurring in both final and non-final tonics in sentences. In this case other prosodic and paralinguistic features are excluded (Table 5.5).

Tone	Position in sentence	Descriptive label
level	final tonic in sentence	*absence of emotional involvement*, which may be interpreted as sarcasm, irony, boredom, etc.
	non-final tonic in sentence	*implication of routineness* – perhaps arising out of the level tone in final position
low rise	final tonic in sentence	*personal inconclusiveness* – specific labels used here are non-committal, unaggressive, etc., which are a short remove from polite, respectful, etc.
		social openness – specific labels used here are casual, friendly, persuasive, etc. and (with appropriate kinesic accompaniment) warning, grim, etc.
	non-final tonic in sentence	*attitudinally neutral*
low fall	final tonic in sentence	*attitudinally neutral*
	non-final tonic in sentence	*personal definitiveness* – specific labels used here are abrupt, insistent, etc.
		unsociability – specific labels being cool, irritated, rude, etc.
high fall	in any position	*definite emotional commitment* – specific labels being emphasis, surprise, warmth, selection depending very much on kinesic accompaniment
high rise	in any position	*definite emotional inquiry* – specific labels being query, puzzlement, surprise, etc.
fall-rise	in any position	*uncertain outcome* – doubt, hesitation, etc., leading to suspicion, threatening, etc.
rise-fall	in any position	*definitive outcome* – impressed, satisfied, smug, etc., or the reverse, depending on kinesic accompaniment

TABLE 5.5 Crystal's system (1975)

This second version also recognizes one feature at least of Halliday's description, namely the acknowledgement of neutral forms. But Crystal has confined his attention to pitch movements in the tonic and neglected the wider range of pitch movements in the pre-tonic.

2.5 Brown

Brown (1977) reviewed novelists' descriptions of the way their characters talk and, by comparing the prosodic and paralinguistic features required, produced thirteen categories: *replied/answered/said*; *retorted/exclaimed*; *important/pompous/responsible*; *depressed/miserably/sadly*; *excited*; *anxious/worried/nervous*; *shrill/shriek/scream*; *warmly*; *coldly*; *thoughtfully*; *sexily*; *crossly/angrily*; *queried/echoed*.

Brown's selection of features includes lip setting, but does not specifically include step-up/-down, high unstressed syllables, strong syllables, rhythmicality or 'flattened' tail. She happens to have chosen nine attitudinal categories not covered by Crystal, and only three which are parallel. It is interesting to see that Brown's and Crystal's specifications are almost identical for *excited* and *angry*, but differ markedly for *worried* – indeed Crystal's worried subjects were marked by slow speech, Brown's by rapid speech!

It is highly instructive to examine and compare the prosodic/paralinguistic analysis of emotions as presented by Crystal and Brown. If we extract from their lists those emotions that involve departures from normal pitch level and from normal pitch range, and group them in such a way as to display those departures, we will begin to see general characteristics associated with them (see Table 5.6). Some emotions involve only general pitch level, either high or low: some emotions involve general pitch range, either wide or narrow; other emotions involve various combinations; none in their lists involve the combination of **high and narrow**.

The general characteristics of the departure from normal pitch level seem to reflect the emotional, nervous condition of the speaker. With the high level, the speaker is tense and emotions are aroused, and nervous tension is heightened; with the low level, the speaker is either relaxed ('satisfied', 'important, pompous, responsible'; cf. Pike's gloss 'deliberative') or emotions are constrained or 'reined in' and nervous tension is deflated.

The general characteristics of the departures from normal pitch range seem to display the speaker's relationship to the listener. With a wide range, the speaker is warm and open towards the listener or, at least in the case of *shrill/shriek/scream*, intends to impress the listener of a need for a very definite response. With a narrow range, the speaker is cold towards the listener and may well not be interested in any response.

'High' and 'low', and 'wide' and 'narrow' have been discussed in relation to tones up to this point, but these terms also seem to apply to heads as well.

	Crystal (1969)	Brown (1977)
HIGH	haughty amused worried	anxious, worried, nervous
HIGH and WIDE	puzzled pleased questioning	excited shrill, shriek, scream cross, angry
WIDE	excited	retort, exclaim warm querying, echoing
LOW and WIDE		sexy
LOW	dismayed disapproving vexed conspiratorial impatient satisfied	important, pompous, responsible
LOW and NARROW	grim	depressed
NARROW	bored	cold

TABLE 5.6

Indeed, Crystal's 'step-up' and 'step-down' involve heads, and his 'high unstressed syllables' can only refer to heads. Such reference to heads immediately resolves some apparent anomalies between Crystal's and Brown's analysis. For instance, Crystal does not credit *excited* with high, but only with wide, whereas Brown describes *excited* as both high and wide; however, Crystal does refer to a step-up which can occur in both tone and head – thus, Crystal's and Brown's descriptions are almost identical. Similarly, Crystal does not credit *angry* with 'high' or 'wide', unlike Brown; however he does refer to 'high unstressed syllables', and both agree on other prosodic features like loudness, tempo and tension.

3. Intonational resources for attitudinal meaning

In the review of the five intonation systems described in detail above, we have seen that the speaker's attitude is conveyed by a number of different factors. These factors include the choice of lexis, the actual situation in which the utterance takes place, the choice of other prosodic and paralinguistic features besides those related to intonation, and fourthly, not mentioned hitherto, body gestures, particularly of the face and hands. The fifth factor is intonation.

We are now in a position to present the features of that fifth factor: the intonational resources for attitudinal meaning are: pitch level, range of the tone, different types of heads and the pitch of the pre-head. We already have described in Chapter 4 the neutral forms of the falling, rising and falling-rising tones, which are basic features in the informational, syntactic and communicative functions of intonation. Variations from these neutral forms constitute those features of intonation that are used for the expression of the attitudinal function.

Similarly, there are neutral forms of head and a neutral form of the pre-head, and variations from these forms are also used for the expression of the attitudinal function of intonation.

3.1   Variations in tones

If the fall starts from a pitch level above mid-high, it is called a **high fall**; if the fall starts from approximately mid-low, it is called a **low fall**. Thus, there is a threefold classification of falls, which happens to be identical to Halliday's distinction between medium (neutral), wide and narrow, which was illustrated as follows:

1	medium [neutral]	╲
1+	wide	╲
1-	narrow	╲

(Halliday, 1970: 15)

This is parallel also to Pike's classification of falls: high (1–4) and low (3–4), beside the 'moderate' fall (2–4). Brown's is also similar – although the distinction is spread over two features, viz. pitch span, and placing in voice range. However, this threefold classification of falls stands in contradistinction to many other analyses which posit only two types of fall (O'Connor and Arnold; Crystal); the main point of contention against such analyses is their unwillingness to acknowledge a full range of neutral forms.

Just as we assert three forms of a falling tone, we also assert three forms of a rising tone. Besides the neutral rise that ends at mid/mid-high level, there are also the **low rise** that ends at mid-low level and the **high rise** that ends above mid-high. It is only Pike who also acknowledges such a three-fold distinction in rises: 4–3 ('deliberative'), 4–2 ('sequences') and 4–1 ('intense'). (It must also be noted that Pike acknowledges other rises too, with a mid-low start (3–2 'questions', 3–1 questions plus 'intensity') and a mid-high start (2–1 'politeness').) All other analyses offer just two forms of rise, whether they are credited as two distinct neutral types (Halliday) or simply as high and low varieties of a rise (O'Connor and Arnold; Crystal, 1975).

The phonetic basis of the threefold classification of rises is the end point of the rise, rather than the starting-point. It is observed that the actual starting-point of the high rise can vary quite considerably, as Pike's analysis highlights; but similarly, the end point of a fall can vary considerably too; again, Pike's analysis highlights this (falls include 1-2, 1-3, 2-3 as well as those falling to 4).

The **high fall** is variously glossed as 'intense', 'unexpected' (Pike), 'personal concern, involvement, liveliness ... more emotional, etc.' (O'Connor and Arnold), 'vigorous agreement or contradiction ... strong surprise, etc.' (Gimson, 1989), 'strong', 'unexpected' (Halliday), 'surprise/redundancy contour' – which includes a low but ascending head (Liberman; 'redundancy' in the sense that the speaker is protesting that the informational content of the message should be regarded as self evident). There is general agreement about the meaning of this intonational form, and we could adopt the label 'strong' or 'intense' – leaving the particular attitude to be specified from lexical and situational factors, e.g. surprise, personal concern, etc. It is tempting to use Brown's description of a high fall as 'an indicator [of] some positive attitude' (Brown, 1977: 129). But since she concedes that the surprise may be either excited or disagreeable, then 'positive' does not seem to be quite so appropriate.

The **low fall** too has a variety of glosses: 'mild', 'detached' (Pike); 'cool, calm, phlegmatic, detached, reserved, dispassionate, dull', 'possibly grim, surly' (O'Connor and Arnold; and Liberman concurs); 'detached, unexcited, dispassionate' (Cruttenden). Again, there is very strong general agreement about the meaning of this intonational form; we could safely adopt the label 'mild' and leave the specification of attitude to the lexical choice and circumstantial features of an utterance.

The **high rise**, i.e. rise to high, receives the same gloss from Pike as the high fall: 'intense', 'unexpected'. However, most other analyses draw attention to its use as echoes, challenges and requests for repetition (O'Connor and Arnold, Halliday, Brown, Crystal); Palmer also characterizes its meaning as 'animated', and Gimson as 'eagerness, brightness, enthusiasm, excitement, concern, indignation'. Again, we could adopt the label 'intense' to indicate the meaning of this intonational form and leave the closer specification of attitude to the accompanying lexical choice and circumstantial features of an utterance.

The **low rise**, i.e. rise to mid-low, must be carefully differentiated from the neutral rise, i.e. rise to mid/mid-high. The latter is very widely termed the 'low rise', when no difference is suggested between it and a 'true' low rise. Yet the meaning of the rise to mid-low is often indicated in the course of description of low rises in general: cf. O'Connor and Arnold: 'reserving judgement', 'guarded', 'reproving criticism', 'resentful contradictions', 'deprecatory', 'wondering', 'calm, casual acknowledgement'; also Cruttenden (1986: 105-6): 'uncertainty', 'non-committal or even grumbling'. Adapting an example from Cruttenden (ibid.), we can illustrate the different meanings of the three rises:

(5.14)   He's \underline{\passed} | \'\underline{hasn't} he (high rise: intense, surprise, challenging,
          'I would be surprised to hear otherwise')

(5.15)   He's \underline{\passed} | /\underline{hasn't} he (neutral rise: question,
          seeking confirmation, 'I would like to be sure')

(5.16)   He's \underline{\passed} | /hasn't he (low rise: non-committal, grumbling,
          'Well, let him be thankful for that at least – he could have failed!')

It seems that most of the attitudes associated with this low rise are negative in some way, but the term 'negative' would be misleading as a label for this intonational form (cf. Brown's observations on the high fall as 'disagreeably surprised', above). Pike characterized this form as 'deliberative'. It means that the speaker is carefully considering the matter in hand. It does not state whether the judgement is favourable or unfavourable - that must be gathered from the context (Pike, 1945: 54). His is an approach very much in line with the approach taken here, but 'deliberative' is too positive a label for its typical use in British English. Cruttenden's label 'non-committal' seems to be the closest we can get to a general label, if it is understood that it includes negative 'signals' regarding the information or the addressee; specific interpretations such as 'menacing', 'disapproving', 'sceptical', would depend, as above, on lexical and situational factors.

The **rise-fall** has two varieties, although it is only Kingdon and Halliday who have distinguished between them. The high rise-fall involves a rise from about mid level to high followed by a fall. The low rise-fall involves a rise from low/mid-low level to about mid pitch followed by a fall. In both cases, the rise element carries the main force (see Halliday, 1970:11); and the total pitch movement can be confined to a single syllable or 'split' over several syllables, in which case the highest point in pitch is usually reached in the syllable following the tonic syllable.

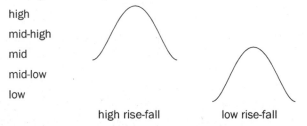

high
mid-high
mid
mid-low
low

          high rise-fall   low rise-fall

The **high rise-fall** is acknowledged in most British studies and is glossed variously as 'intensified' (Palmer), 'enthusiasm, doubt, horror, sarcasm, indignation', etc. (Gimson), 'impressed, awed', 'echoing', 'complacent, self-satisfied, even smug', etc. (O'Connor and Arnold), 'special emphasis' (Kingdon), 'committed', 'insistent', 'asserting' (Halliday), 'definite outcome – impressed, satisfied, smug, etc., or the reverse, depending on kinesic accompaniment' (Crystal, 1975). Along with most American studies, Pike does not acknowledge the high rise-fall; but Bolinger (1986) does (for Bolinger, it is Profile CA), as 'a sort of intensification' of the fall. 'Intensified' is probably the best label for the high rise-fall, being 'stronger' in expression than the high fall.

The **low rise-fall** is omitted in most studies, but is acknowledged by Kingdon and Halliday;[4] the latter glosses it as 'intense, showing awe ... or disappointment' (Halliday, 1970: 32). He also observes that it is frequently accompanied by breathy voice quality. The best label would seem to be 'intensified, plus emotion', whether that emotion is awe or disappointment, or anything else as indicated by lexical choice and other situational factors. That Halliday[5] readily acknowledges typical accompaniment of other voice qualities (breathiness) is evidence that there is a greater involvement of emotional expression.

There is also a low variety of the fall-rise. The neutral fall-rise, which conveys thematic marking and implication in the informational function of intonation, has a fall from about mid-high pitch to mid or mid-low, followed by a rise. The low fall-rise begins its fall element at about mid pitch and 'it falls more steeply and over a wider range [than the neutral fall-rise], descending to a low pitch' (Halliday, 1970: 18).

The **low fall-rise** is glossed either as 'exclusive, contrastive, expressing strong reservation' (Halliday) or as combining 'incomplete deliberation' with 'mild attention (or contrast)' and 'detached attitude' (Pike). Pike's gloss may well reflect American usage, but Halliday's seems right for British usage. The label 'strongly contrastive/implicational' is thus proposed.

3.2   Heads

It is now time to look at heads in more detail and examine the part they play in the expression of attitudinal meanings. As with tones, it seems necessary to identify neutral forms of heads in order to make a distinction between forms that do and do not carry expressions of attitude. Just as there are neutral forms for both falling and rising tones, there are also neutral forms of heads that accompany the neutral tones. In this respect, we follow the lead that Halliday has taken, and we can adopt much of his description of neutral heads.

Heads may be level, ascending, descending (or mixed or glissando). **Level** heads may be high, mid-high, mid, mid-low, or low; obviously, with instrumental phonetic study it is possible to identify a 'gradience' of pitch levels for heads as it is with pitch levels for the beginning point of tones, but since high, mid and low offer themselves as obvious candidates as pitch heights, and since it is also possible to conceive of intermediate levels between high, mid and low, these five pitch levels form a base from which to describe functionally distinct pitch levels for heads. **Ascending** and **descending** are chosen as labels for heads to maintain a distinction between the movement of pitch in heads and the movement of pitch in tones (i.e. 'falling' and 'rising'). **Glissando** is a term adopted from Crystal's work to refer to 'smooth and usually fairly slow glides' (1969: 164) in pitch which are contained within a head; these are identical to what O'Connor and Arnold called 'sliding' and 'climbing' heads.

There is a fair amount of variation in the actual form of neutral heads. Generally speaking, a neutral head is either level at mid, mid-high or mid-low pitch, or gradually ascends or descends towards the level of the beginning point of the tone. What must be borne in mind at this point, is that the pitch level of the onset syllable is significant in terms of textual structure. Once the onset pitch level has been given, the neutral form of the head then adjusts to the beginning point of the tone, reaching about mid pitch – hence the ascending or descending movement of pitch in the head. When heads involve a number of accented syllables there may well be an arbitrary mixture of ascending and descending syllables. The neutral heads before a neutral fall may be illustrated, therefore, as follows:

mid-level

ascending

descending

mixed   etc.

The neutral heads before a neutral rise may be illustrated likewise, as follows:

mid-level

ascending

descending

mixed

The end point of heads is adjusted slightly before high and low falls, so that the final syllables of the head are fairly close in pitch to the beginning point of the fall.

3.2.1 Low and high heads

A **low level head** before a fall and a **high level head** before a rise have the effect of concentrating attention exclusively on the focus of information. This particular sequencing is not acknowledged by Halliday, but Pike makes reference to the effect, at least, of the low level head before a fall:

> precontour four [= low level head] heightens the contrastive pointing of any succeeding falling primary contour by making a relatively large interval between the precontour and the beginning of the primary contour; the greater the interval, the sharper the contrast or pointing and attention.   (Pike, 1945: 66)

Pike does not offer any similar observation about the 'inverted' sequence of high level head and rising tone, but the effect is, in fact, identical. In each case, the focus is highlighted, at the expense of the semantic value of the 'given' section of the intonation unit. They can be illustrated as follows:

low head   _____⌐\   before a fall

high head   _____⌐/   before a rise

A high level head may also precede a fall, and a low level head may precede a rise. The latter is specifically incorporated by Halliday into his description of English under the label 'involvement':

> Involvement may mean a desire to affect the decision, thus implying suggestion or encouragement, or may imply some judgment as 'you ought (not) to', 'you should have told me'.   (Halliday, 1967: 44)

The low level head before a low rise (as opposed to before a neutral rise) features in O'Connor and Arnold's description of English (pattern 3). The low narrow rise mixes the 'relaxed, deflated, deliberative' meaning with a 'cold' relationship towards the listener, thus producing the 'non-committal' attitude; however, the low level head adds involvement, and the whole combination produces the kind of effect that O'Connor and Arnold have described in the following terms: reserving judgement, reproving criticism, resentful contradiction, disapproving, menacing, scepticism – a rather unpleasant catalogue of attitudes, augmented by Halliday's 'unconcern' and 'uncertainty'.

The low level head before a high rise seems to express incredulity and disbelief, mixing involvement with aroused emotions and a 'warm' relationship with the listener – at least in the sense that the utterance is likely to produce a definite reaction from the listener.

The low level head before rises can be illustrated as follows:

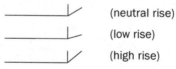

_____/   (neutral rise)

_____⌐/   (low rise)

_____/   (high rise)

The high level head before falls has a similar effect; Pike refers to 'insistence' and 'unexpectedness'. It is neater to refer to all this as 'involvement' again, but to note the variations as a result of the combination with neutral, high and low falls.

Cruttenden observes a sense of 'weightiness' when the high level head is combined with a low fall, for instance. The high level head before falls can be illustrated as follows:

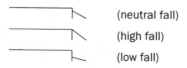

_____\   (neutral fall)

_____\   (high fall)

_____⌐\   (low fall)

3.2.2 *Wide descending and ascending heads*

We now move on to consider another type of head, in which there is a considerable movement of pitch, either descending from high/mid-high to low/mid-low, or ascending from low/mid-low to high/mid-high. The difference between these descending and ascending heads and those that were considered to be variants of the neutral form of head is the degree of pitch movement. This 'non-neutral' form has a wide pitch range, and may be conveniently referred to as the **wide descending/ascending** head. Both possibilities can occur before both falling and rising tones.

The general effect of the wide descending head is a combination of the meaning of **wide** (warm relationship with the listener or, at least, a strong expectation of some kind of response) with one meaning of **fall**, viz. authority. This agrees well with Pike's gloss 'insistent'. Other glosses include – with a following fall – 'categoric, considered, weighty, judicial, dispassionate; often withdrawal, impatience' (with statements), 'searching, serious, intense, responsible, often impatience, irritability' (with *wh*-questions), 'more ponderous; often impatient' (with *yes/no* questions), 'firm, serious, considered, weighty, pressing, dispassionate' (with commands), and 'great weight, emphasis' (with exclamations) (all from O'Connor and Arnold).

Again, this plethora of attitudes can be sorted out by reference to lexical and situational factors, but the general meaning is as given above: warm relationship with listener and/or strong expectation of response, with a degree of authority, together with whatever is signified by the kind of tone that follows – either falling or rising.[6]

The wide ascending head combines the general meaning of **wide** with one of the meanings of **rise**, viz. appeal to the listener. Palmer has a general gloss for this head (which he calls 'scandent'):

As compared with a Superior Head (= high level head), the Scandent Head generally expresses more animation. Compare the impressive:

⁻sʌdnli ðei sɔ: θri: inɔ:məs ↘ wulvz!

with the vivacious:

ˊsʌdnli ðei sɔ: θri: inɔ:məs ↘ wulvz!

The first sentence implies: 'How horror-struck they must have been! What a terrible situation for them!'
    The second sentence implies rather: 'How surprised they must have been! What an interesting experience for them!'

(Palmer, 1922: 76–7)

Note that Palmer is careful not to label this head as 'vivacious', or 'petulant', for the precise attitude or emotion depends on the lexical and

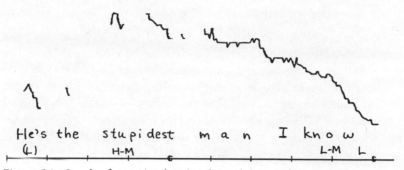

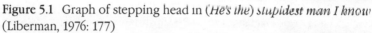

Figure 5.1 Graph of stepping head in (*He's the*) *stupidest man I know* (Liberman, 1976: 177)

situational factors of an utterance. However, both Pike and O'Connor and Arnold describe the combination of wide ascending head and a falling tone as expressing protests. This fits in well with the general meaning adduced above, as protests indeed involve a strong expectation of some kind of response, an appeal and a statement of fact, belief or reality.[7]

3.2.3 *Stepping heads*

O'Connor and Arnold use the term 'stepping head' for a wide descending head in which the stressed syllable of each accented word is a step lower in pitch than the previous one (1973: 73); the 'stepping' adds a sense of emphasis to what the speaker is saying. Liberman (1979: 174-7) does not seem to acknowledge this, but accepts it as simply a variation of the more normal falling movement. However, Pike recognizes the distinction: his 'descending stress series' is equivalent to the stepping head, and its meaning is given as 'intense precision, or certainty'.

A very clear picture of the stepping head is provided by Liberman, despite the above comment: Figure 5.2 shows the movement of pitch in the utterance *(He's the) stupidest man I know*.

The graph shows the 'stepping' very clearly, as opposed to a smoother descending pitch movement. This type of head is best depicted as:

but it can also precede a rise:

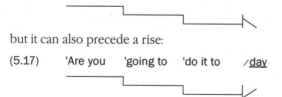

with the same degree of emphasis.

Pike and O'Connor and Arnold only conceive of 'stepping heads' as stepping downwards; but stepping heads can step upwards too (see Crystal, 1969: 230). The stepping effect simply adds an extra degree of emphasis to the meanings of the wide ascending heads and is strongly related to another quite independent prosodic feature, viz. degree of loudness of the accented syllable. The ascending stepping head is depicted as follows:

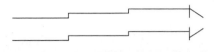

3.2.4 Glissando heads

Glissando takes the additional degree of emphasis a stage further. Glissando involves a pitch movement, or a series of pitch movements, either descending or ascending, **before** a tonic syllable, i.e. within a head; if a series of pitch movements are involved, the pitch movement is constant throughout the head and is dependent on accented syllables with noticeable rhythmicality. The difference between a glissando movement and a tonic movement is a matter of prominence.[8]

Glissando may involve a descending movement or an ascending movement, or a series of each, but never mixed. The pitch level of the beginning point of each descending movement may remain constant throughout the head, but it may also gradually fall (Crystal, 1969: 221; Ladd, 1983). No such observation is made by Crystal or Ladd (or Halliday, for that matter) for the reverse possibility: a gradual rise in the pitch level of the beginning point of each ascending movement; but it is not inconceivable.

Halliday describes glissando heads as 'bouncing', 'uneven' and 'swinging'. Before a falling tone, he acknowledges glissando ascending ('uneven') pre-tonics (heads), but not glissando descending. Before a low pitched rise-fall, he also acknowledges only glissando ascending ('a swinging movement with ... each foot rising ...', 1970: 19); in fact, he takes this kind of head to be the only possible head before a low-pitched fall-rise.

It seems to me that there is a 'gradience' of meaning distinctions between descending heads, stepping descending heads and glissando descending heads. As we have noted above, the descending head indicates a warm relationship with the listener or, at least, a strong expectation of some kind of response, with a tone of authority. The stepping effect adds emphasis to this; the glissando effect adds forcefulness – conceding no opportunity for contradiction. Compare the following utterances with each of three types of head:

(5.18)   The sun rises in the <u>east</u>

(5.19)   It is time for you to go to <u>bed</u>

(a)   with a wide descending head: authoritatively
(b)   with a stepping descending head: authoritatively, and emphatically
(c)   with a glissando descending head: authoritatively, and forcefully

The glissando ascending lacks the sense of authority, but includes a sense of appeal, a sense of demanding that something should be taken into account. Halliday's example was

(5.20)   He 'simply 'doesn't under\underline{stand}

(1967: 42)

glossed as 'insistent'; however, the effect of the glissando ascending head is more like 'I appeal to you to believe my estimation of him'. The two utterances given above ((5.18), (5.19)) can also be rendered with glissando ascending heads, with a meaning like 'I appeal to you to remember what I've told you ten times already' (or 'I appeal to you to think it out logically', etc.), expressed forcefully.

Halliday did not consider the possibility of glissando heads before a rising tone, but Gimson did. The note of authority with forcefulness, or appeal with forcefulness, is obviously combinable with the elicitation of information, open suasion, etc. Examples from Gimson include:

(5.21)   Are you \sure that \George and \Mary /\underline{know}

(5.22)   \Mind you \put your \hat and \coat /\underline{on}

(5.23)   /Will you be /coming to /see us on /\underline{Mon}day?

(5.24)   /Don't make /such a /\underline{noise}

(Gimson, 1989: 285)

(NB: Other examples of Gimson's remind us that all those different kinds of heads may precede a variety of tones, including the fall-rise.)

The glissando heads can be depicted as follows:

\ \ \ ∧   \ \ \ ⋁   (glissando descending)

/ / / ∧·   / / / ⋁   (glissando ascending)

3.3   Pre-heads

Finally, we turn to pre-heads, the sequence of relatively unaccented syllables before the onset syllable, or before the tonic syllable if there is no separate onset syllable. Analyses vary quite considerably in the amount of attention given to pre-heads. On the one hand, Halliday does not recognize a distinction between head and pre-head at all, assigning both to an undifferentiated 'pre-tonic segment'. Pike did not spare much space for the consideration of what he called 'proprecontour' (1945: 68) and which he described as 'introductory to the more important precountour' (= head) (ibid.); it is usually pitched low, at level 4 or 3, many examples of it being found scattered through his whole description. On the other hand, Crystal (1969) distinguishes between five types of pre-head, Liberman distinguishes between three, and O'Connor and Arnold merely between high and low pre-heads.

O'Connor and Arnold seem to consider the low pre-head as normal – it is not indicated by any transcription symbol; but the high pre-head is said to indicate emphasis (O'Connor and Arnold, 1973: 36). It is illustrated by their pair:

(5.25)   The \fool

(5.26)   ⁻The \fool

where the high pre-head in (5.26) makes 'the whole utterance more exclamatory, more emphatic ...' (1973: 36). There is certainly an extra dimension added to the meaning by the adoption of a high pre-head instead of a low one, and it does seem surprising that Halliday has neglected this little bit of the intonation system completely.

By contrast, Crystal offers a clear and simple classification of five types of pre-head, directly from detailed observation of his corpus (1969: 233–5). The normal pre-head is approximately mid-low pitch, 'a little below that of the onset syllable', which is given, typically, as mid. The high pre-head is pitched above the level of the onset, and the extra-high pre-head above that again. The mid pre-head is heard as being on the same pitch level as the onset, and the extra-low pre-head is 'below normal low level'. But Crystal does not venture any meaning attached to any of these varieties, although he did note that high unstressed syllables in the pre-head feature in his category 'amused'.

There is general agreement that a pre-head at mid/mid-low level is a neutral form in that it does not carry any expression of attitude. The neutral form is, in fact, strongly influenced by the pitch level of the onset; it may be higher than mid before high onset, and lower than mid before low onset. Variations from this neutral form do carry meaning, however, and the meaning is generally very simple. Most cases of the 'marked' pre-heads involve a pitch contrast with the immediately following onset syllable, or, in the case of 'head-less' intonation units, with the immediately following tonic syllable: low pre-head before high onset or high beginning of a falling tone; high pre-head before low onset or low beginning of a rising tone. And the meaning is identical to those cases of high heads before rises and low heads before falls: it directs particular attention to the informational content of the head, or, in the case of 'head-less' units, to the focus. Additional specification of the attitude must be provided by the lexical content and the situational factors relating to the utterances; what the 'marked' low/high pre-head does is simply to indicate that the utterance is marked attitudinally.

———

4. Summary

The attitudinal potential in English intonation can be summarized as follows:

4.1 Tones

There are neutral forms of falling, rising and falling-rising tones, whose meanings are determined by the informational, syntactic and communicative functions of intonation. The falling and rising tones both have **high** and **low** varieties which are, thereby, attitudinally marked; high is 'strong/intense', low is 'mild' with falls, and 'non-committal' with rises. The falling tone has further varieties: **rise-falls**, which can be either high, meaning 'stronger/more intense' (than the high fall), or **low**, meaning 'intensified, plus emotional'. The fall-rise has a neutral form which is high, and an attitudinally marked form which is **low**, meaning 'strongly contrastive/ implicational'.

	Neutral	Marked	Meaning
A	**Tones**		
	fall \	high '	strong, intense
		low \	mild
		high rise-fall ∧	stronger, more intense
		low rise-fall ∧	intensified, plus emotional
	rise /	high /	strong, intense
		low /	non-committal
	fall-rise ∨	low ∨	strongly contrastive/ implicational
B	**Heads/pre-heads**		
	mid level		
		pitch contrast high ⁻ (before rise) low ₋ (before fall)	highlighting information
		high ⁻ (before fall) low ₋ (before rise)	insistent involved
		descending (wide) \	warm/expectation of response; authority
		ascending (wide) /	warm/expectation of response; appeal
		stepping \' /'	emphatic
		glissando \\ //	forceful

TABLE 5.7   Neutral and attitudinal marked tones and heads/pre-heads

4.2 Heads and pre-heads

As with tones, there are neutral forms of heads and pre-heads, which have no independent meaning from that indicated by the tone involved. Pitch contrast is brought about by the combinations of low head/pre-head with fall, high head/pre-head with rise, low pre-head with high onset, and high pre-head with low onset meaning 'highlighting the immediately following informational content', either in the head, or in the tonic. Descending heads/pre-heads, if they are wide, mean 'warm relationship with listener and/or strong expectation of response, with an authoritative tone'; ascending heads/pre-heads, if they are wide, mean 'warm relationship with listener and/or strong expectation of response, with a note of appeal to the listener'. Stepping heads, both descending and ascending, add emphasis, and glissandi, again both descending and ascending, add forcefulness.

Notes

1. The tonic actually begins in the middle of *x*: /eg\zæmz/. The orthographical version could read *ex\xams*, if it is felt necessary that this point should be made clear.

2. Note that O'Connor and Arnold use labels from communicative functions for the five different clause types.

3. Brazil's notion of 'termination' also exploits this variation in degree of fall (Brazil, 1975, 1978).

4. Pike does acknowledge the low rise-fall (4-3-4), but notes that it may be accompanied by harshness and suggests 'repudiation' as its meaning. But that meaning seems to be tied to the solitary example he gives:

No,	oh no,	that can't be true	
°4-3-4 |	1- °4-3-4|	°2- -4-3	(Pike, 1945: 57)

   The same intonational sequence with *Yes, yes, that must be so* could easily yield the meaning 'acceptance'.

5. And Pike (see n. 4).

6. The glosses that Schubiger (1958) provides for the combination of wide descending head with a rising tone are quite illuminating and bring out the effect of the rise: 'friendly, reassuring, encouraging' (with statements); 'rather complaining; tone of entreaty' (i.e. strong expectation of response, plus request) (with commands); 'resentful, reproachful, perplexed' (with *wh*-questions); 'entreaty, despair, concern' (with *yes/no* questions); and 'tenderness' (with exclamations, e.g. *Good old London*):

   (5.27)   Good old /London

   (see Schubiger, 1958: 57)

7. It is only Palmer and Schubiger who isolate the combination of wide ascending head with a rising tone for any comment: for Palmer it represented a more animated form of *yes/no* question, besides echo questions and statements; for Schubiger, it meant 'patronizing, condescending' if the rising tone was low (e.g. Lady (to charwoman, on Boxing Day):

   (5.28)   Come into the /drawing room

8. For a full discussion of the problems of identification, see Crystal (1969: 221-2).

6

Intonation in a model of communication

1. Models of communication

It has been the interest of many linguists to construct a model of the processes by which we communicate with each other. In the simplest terms, we can construct a flow-chart diagram that shows the direction of activities from a sender to a receiver, the co-ordination of brain and voice (or hands, in the case of written communication) of the sender, and of ear (or eyes, in the case of written communication) and brain of the receiver, and the physical substance by which the communication is transmitted – sound through the air, or marks (writing) on material (like paper).

However, there are other factors involved. One factor, of course, is the language or dialect (or languages or dialects) in which the communication is to be conveyed; secondly, the sender takes into account a number of other factors in the context of the proposed communication. One such factor is the receiver, or receivers: we adjust the form of a communication on account of how old the receiver is, whether we know them and how well we know them, whether we like them, how many there are of them, and so on. We also take into account where we are and where they are, i.e. the physical settings, the atmosphere of the encounter, i.e. the 'scene', and also the channel by which we will communicate: face to face, by phone, by letter, etc. Also, our psychological state affects the way we communicate; if we feel angry, we will sound angry, and that could well affect our choice of vocabulary and the pitch of our voice. A fourth factor is the purpose of the communication; telling somebody off sounds quite different from advice; advice is different from suggesting a course of action, which itself is different from a recommendation, etc.; this aspect of communication was dealt with in Chapter 4; it clearly involves intonation as well as grammatical and lexical choices. A fifth factor is the context of the communication both at a macro and a micro level; a communication is sent in the context of what the sender knows and what the sender thinks the receiver knows; the context also involves what has just been said (or written) by either of the participants. The sense of context might also be broadened to include the communication event itself; we adjust the wording and intonation of a communication to be appropriate for different kinds of events: for example, we communicate in one way in the context of a cosy chat with a close friend, and in quite a different way when addressing a stranger, or a crowd, or a panel of examiners, or a very important person.

Thus a model of communication has to not only account for the linguistic processes but also these sociolinguistic factors. In seeking to place intonation in a model of communication, we are thereby looking at intonation's role, or roles, in more general terms than the details specified in the preceding chapters. In order to do that, we must consider the general features of linguistic communication.

Halliday (1973, 1978; see also Halliday and Hasan, 1985) distinguishes between three metafunctions of language: the ideational, the interpersonal and the textual. These are different dimensions of meaning that always feature in any instance of the use of language. The **ideational** encompasses both experiential and logical meanings. **Experiential** meaning refers to the kind of meaning that language possesses for representing our perception of the real world, whereas **logical** meaning refers to the types of relationship between items (e.g. between nouns, or clauses, etc.). For instance, in the following utterance,

There's a cup of tea in the pot if you want one

we know what the words and clauses refer to (experiential meaning) and we recognize the relationship of the second clause to the first – a pragmatic condition (logical meaning).

The **interpersonal** meaning refers to the interaction between the sender and the receiver. In this case, the sender provides some information that is clearly designed to be of benefit to the receiver, and it is quite likely that the receiver will interpret the utterance as an offer. Thus a likely follow-up is the action of pouring tea into a cup. Interpersonal meaning is thus a quite different dimension to the ideational meanings.

The **textual** meaning refers to the way an utterance is worded, organized and intoned to fit into its linguistic environment. The pronoun *one* is used as a substitute for *a cup of tea* to avoid unnecessary repetition. The context provides the basis of the interpretation.

You will no doubt recognize some of the roles that intonation plays in these different functions. Tonality provides the basis for the distribution of information and is often crucial for disambiguating potential clashes of meaning (Chapter 2). Tone is crucial in the interpersonal function (Chapter 4). Tonicity is crucial in the textual function, with its systems of identifying new and given information (Chapter 3).

Thus the illustrative utterance above is likely to be intoned as

(6.1)   There's a cup of tea in the \pot | if you /want one

i.e. two pieces of information, one major, the other minor; a statement (the falling tone); all new information in the first unit (broad focus), given information (*one*) in the second as well as new (*if you want*).

But there are other ways of formulating that statement. Joos, in a famous and entertaining work (Joos, 1961), attempted to disabuse people of the impression that a language is a monolithic, unchanging, construct. His *Five Clocks* presented five distinct styles of communication. The above utterance was communicated by a male to a group of three women whom he did not know, in a setting that was unfamiliar to both himself and them. This is a typical situation for what Joos called the **consultative** style: the participants in the event do not know each other well, and the group has an upper limit of about six or seven. The speaker has to provide a good deal of background information. In a more **casual** style, the participants know each other and do not need to furnish as much background information; the speaker can rely on 'insider' knowledge, and might render the above as

(6.2)   D'you want a cup of /tea

Intimate style is even more informal and is characterized by what Joos called extraction: 'the speaker extracts a minimum pattern from some conceivable casual sentence' (1961: 30). In this case, the participants know each other so well there is hardly any need to provide background information. This can be illustrated with

(6.3)   cup o'/tea

(or even *Cuppa?*)

Besides these informal styles, more formal ones are also recognized. If the speaker addresses a group that is too large for the consultative style, then a **formal** style is adopted:

(6.4)   You can get yourselves a cup of /tea | in the room next \door

In a formal style, the speaker does not expect the hearers to engage in a conversation or discussion, and has to provide full background information.

Finally, Joos described a **frozen** style 'for print and for declamation ... the reader or the hearer is not permitted to cross-question the author' (1961: 39). The announcement, spoken by a person in authority at a gathering of people,

(6.5)   Tea will be served in the large \lounge | at three forty \five could as well be printed in the programme!

Throughout his study, Joos hints at the role of intonation in defining these styles but offers no detailed descriptions. It is also noticeable, from a phonological point of view, that precision of articulation contributes to the definition of these styles, as the orthographic versions of (6.1), (6.2) and (6.3) testify.

Each of these styles accompanies a different kind of situation. A term used frequently in linguistic study to refer to varieties of situations is **context of situation**. Halliday has been largely responsible for the theoretical development of this term (see Halliday, McIntosh and Strevens, 1964; Halliday, 1973, 1978; and Halliday and Hasan, 1985). He has identified three general headings to describe the features of a situation that go beyond Joos's early attempt. They are the field, the tenor and the mode of discourse.

1 The **field of discourse** refers to what is happening, to the nature of the social action that is taking place: what is it that the participants are engaged in, in which language figures as some essential component?

2 The **tenor of discourse** refers to who is taking part, to the nature of the participants, their statuses and roles: what kinds of role relationship obtain among the participants, including permanent and temporary relationships of one kind or another, both the types of speech role that they are taking on in the dialogue and the whole cluster of socially significant relationships in which they are involved?

3 The mode of discourse refers to what part the language is playing, what it is that the participants are expecting the language to do for them in that situation: the symbolic organisation of the text, the status that it has, and its function in the context, including the channel (is it spoken or written or some combination of the two?) and also the rhetorical mode, what is being achieved by the text in terms of such categories as persuasive, expository, didactic, and the like.

(Halliday and Hasan, 1985: 12)

Every instance of the use of language, however long or short, can be analysed in terms of its field, tenor and mode.

A more explicit instrument for the description of instances of the use of language (or speech acts) is provided in the work of the anthropologist Hymes (see, for instance, Hymes, 1977). He identifies the following components:

1 **Message form**, the actual choice of lexis, syntax, phonology/ orthography with accompanying phonetic or graphic detail; compare, for instance, the different wordings of (6.1) to (6.5).

2 **Message content**, the topic, which happened to be the same for (6.1) to (6.5).

3 **Setting**, the time and place of a speech act, its physical circumstances.

4 **Scene**, the 'psychological setting', or cultural definition of an occasion as a certain type of scene, e.g. a wedding, or a wedding reception, or a best man's speech, or a toast to the bridesmaids, or a tea-break, etc.

5 **Participants**, the speaker/sender/addressor and the hearer/receiver/audience/addressee, their respective ages, genders, statuses, relationships.

6 **Ends**, both the conventionally recognized and expected outcomes from a community perspective and the goals of the individuals involved, e.g. the public recognition of a marriage and the promises taken individually by the bride and groom.

7 **Key**, the tone, manner or spirit in which an act is done, e.g. willingly, grudgingly, as practice, etc. Hymes adds: 'The significance of key is underlined by the fact that, when it is in conflict with the overt content of an act, it often overrides the latter (as in sarcasm). The signalling of key may be non-verbal, as with a wink ...' (Hymes, 1977: 58). (It may also be intonational, either linguistic or paralinguistic.)

8 **Channels**, the choice of oral, written, manual (as in sign language) and other means of transmission.

9 **Forms of speech**, dialects, accents, registers, speech styles as, for instance, when a speaker switches to a different accent (including intonation) to initiate a humorous comment or anecdote.

10 **Norms of interaction**, the rules that determine specific behaviour and proprieties in a speech act or event, e.g. when it is not acceptable to interrupt or speak aloud, when it is acceptable to heckle or cheer (e.g. in a best man's speech).

11 **Genres**, a conventionally recognized type of language event that is identified by a unique combination of linguistic forms, thus enabling members of a community to distinguish between, for example, newsreading and other formal, solo, performances to an audience such as recitations, sermons, announcements, etc., and between conversations and debates, etc. The notion of prosodic composition (see Chapter 1) is important in this respect.

The description of the situation can also be approached from a socio-psychological perspective, seeking to understand a given situation and its development from the 'actor's-eye-view' (Brown and Fraser, 1979: 56). Giles and Coupland (1991: 13–20) report on studies of people's perceptions of social situations in which five dimensions emerge: co-operative–competitive; intense–superficial; formal–informal; dominant–equal; task-orientated–non-task-orientated. This is clearly a more elaborate system than Joos's, but just as Joos considered intonation as one of the pieces of linguistic evidence for different styles, Giles and Hewstone (1982) took phonological and phonetic factors into account when speculating on the potential speech patterns deriving from people's assessment of a situation. Their chart of

	A	B	C	D
Objective characteristics of certain typical social situations (e.g., A–D)	Friends chatting during coffee break	Prosecuting and defence lawyers in law court	Welsh and English rugby supporters in pub after international match with mutually satisfactory result	Trade union and management negotiation crisis
Possible cognitive structures of social situations by participants	**A1** Interindividual encounter Co-operative Informal Relaxed Equal Not task-related	**B1** Interindividual encounter Competitive Formal Tense Not equal Task-related	**C1** Intergroup encounter Co-operative Informal Relaxed Equal Not task-related	**D1** Intergroup encounter Competitive Formal Tense Not equal Task-related
Potential speech patterns	**A2** Low linguistic diversity 'Restricted' code Verbal style **Non-standard pronunciations** **Imprecise enunciations** First name and informal address forms	**B2** High linguistic diversity 'Elaborated' code Nominal style **Standard pronunciations** **Precise enunciations** Title and/or last name address forms	**C2** Low linguistic diversity 'Restricted' code Verbal style **Non-standard pronunciations** **Imprecise enunciations** First name and informal address forms Attenuation of ingroup speech markers (speech convergence)	**D2** High linguistic diversity 'Elaborated' code Nominal style **Standard pronunciations** **Precise enunciations** Title and/or last name address forms Accentuation of ingroup speech markers (speech divergence)

TABLE 6.1 Towards a model of speech as a dependent variable of social situations (from Giles and Hewstone, 1982: 220)

sample situations is reproduced in Table 6.1 with the phonological and phonetic factors highlighted; intonation could have featured too.

Finally in this review of the 'ingredients' of communication, we look at the lexico-grammatical component of Fawcett's (1980) model of an interacting mind. Fawcett divides up Halliday's three metafunctions into eight functional components that, incidentally, help to identify the roles of intonation; but in addition, he adds two further components. The first is for those bits of language that help in expressing discourse organization, to indicate a specific addressee or nominate the next turn-taker or indicate the sequencing of information (e.g. *firstly, on the one hand*). The second is metalanguage, as when a person overtly monitors their form of expression by glossing (*or in other words*), reformulation, appeals (*you know what I mean?*), and so on.

Halliday's metafunctions	Fawcett's functional components
ideational	experiential logical relationships negativity
interpersonal	interactional affective modality
textual	thematic informational
	discourse organizational metalingual

TABLE 6.2

A speaker negotiates all ten kinds of meaning simultaneously, although the last two are redundant unless they are marked overtly.

The value of Fawcett's interacting mind model is that it draws attention to other components essential to the process of communication. The communication itself draws upon a person's knowledge of the real world, including the addressee's presumed knowledge, and the person's affective state. The communication is often supplemented by other semiotic codes, like gestures, eye contact, physical distance, and intonational paralanguage. The speaker often has a plan of communication, e.g. how to counter an expected argument; but the plan may also involve a staging strategy; what to say first, how to follow it up, etc. in blocks of information equivalent to written paragraphs. Fawcett calls this kind of planning the 'discourse construction program'. And finally, Fawcett acknowledges that a communication can be accompanied by 'non-communicational behavioural programs': 'The point of including this is to remind ourselves that not all options in behaviour necessarily involve communicating with another member of our species, or any type of communication at all' (Fawcett, 1980: 62-3).

We are now in a position to take an actor's-eye-view of the communication process and in order to make the process clear, the first person singular will be used, so that you can identify with it.

A need arises for me to say something. (By using the word *say* it is not intended that writing is excluded; indeed the expression *write down just what you want to say* indicates that saying is not confined to the oral medium.)

I have at my disposal my language and a certain competence in it. I have a stock of words (my lexicon) that I am confident in employing, but also I acknowledge an acquaintance with other words with which I am not so confident, and other words that I do not really understand. My active lexicon is considerably smaller than the total stock of words available in English. I am aware not only of the denotations of my active lexicon but also their connotations, associations and collocations. I am also aware of differences between standard and non-standard (dialectal) usages of some words and the appropriateness of some words to a particular register. I have a stock of syntactical patterns for the deployment of my total active lexicon and a list of morphological shapes of the words for particular syntactic environments. I am also aware that a few of those morphological shapes have variants in my idiolect, e.g. the plural of *formula* as either *formulas* or *formulae*, the past tense of *kneel* as either *knelt* or *kneeled*. I know how to link words and syntactic patterns with each other to produce coherent discourse. I have a pronunciation system which enables me to articulate every single word I wish to use, and every phrase, and every utterance; the system includes consonants, vowels/diphthongs, syllable structures, word stress, rhythm and intonation. I also have variations in the system for rhetorical effect (like joking in a non-standard accent) and for social effect, accommodating to or disaccommodating from those I happen to be addressing. I have a script (alphabet), a spelling and a punctuation system to record what I want to say in writing.

I may also have a second (or third, etc.) language in which I am equally confident. However, my competence in a second language may well be distinctly more restricted. This degree of competence will determine my effectiveness in any bilingual or second language situation.

I also have a knowledge of the universe, although I readily concede that I do not know or understand everything. My (imperfect) knowledge extends to an assumption of what my addressee knows and understands. It also includes the context of my culture which enables me to assess most contexts of situations that I encounter. It also provides me with notions of norms of interaction and interpretation and the appropriateness of types of genres for particular occasions. I also readily concede that my knowledge of the universe will diverge in both general and detailed ways from another person's knowledge, that the context of my culture will be different from others', and that I may be mistaken about any assumptions about others'.

In wanting to say something, I draw upon my linguistic competence(s) and my knowledge of the universe. I also decide how much I want to say and what medium I want to use. If I want to say a lot, I will have to plan ahead (discourse construction program); if I have very little to say, then there is very little planning and I will probably proceed in a very *ad hoc* manner, depending on how the situation changes and, in particular, how the topic develops.

I know what I want to say; I recognize the topic. I assess the situation I find myself in, and accordingly decide how I want to word what I want to say. I take into account the physical setting, including the bystanders, and the scene, the social occasion; also the participants, their number (it may be only one participant other than myself, or even just myself in a soliloquy), their age, gender, race, personality, interests, attentiveness, physical appearance and any temporary mood, emotion or attitude, their relationship to me in either a private or public capacity, their relationship with each other if they number more than one, and their attitude towards me, any bystanders, and the topic itself; what I hope to achieve, and what I think that they expect; my feelings, as well as theirs; and what has just been said. All this influences my decision about how I will say what I want to say.

Having assessed the situation, I encode what I want to say to the extent that my competence in the language(s) allows. Particular items of my lexicon are selected; they take particular morphological shapes for their functions in the particular syntactical patterns I selected, which are joined together by particular cohesive ties to form coherent discourse; particular phonological or orthographical items are required; the brain activates particular neural patterns and thus the encoding of the message is performed, by being converted into physical (either acoustic or visual) substance.

That physical substance is transmitted and received by your ear, or eye.

I monitor what I say, and if necessary, adjust it.

You decode, to the extent that your competence in the language(s) allows. Particular items received are matched to your lexicon, grammar, phonology, orthography and discourse competences, and thus, hopefully, a degree of comprehension is achieved. However, some details may not match, e.g. the connotations of a lexical item, the perception of a vowel sound (was it *man* or *men*?), the referent of a pronoun like *those*, etc.

Your comprehension of my message is then affected by your assessment of the situation, along the same lines as above. Your assessment operates as

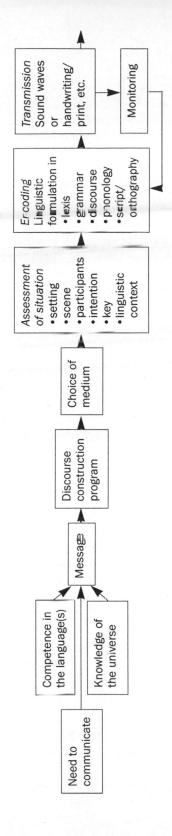
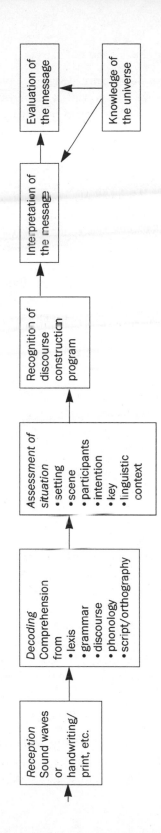

Figure 6.1 A model of the communication process

a filter, producing not just a comprehension of my message, but an interpretation, and, possibly, a response. The interpretation develops as the discourse proceeds. You also evaluate the message you have interpreted; you might agree or disagree, accept it as true or regard it as a lie, consider it interesting or insignificant, etc., but you do so in terms of your knowledge of the universe.

The whole process can be captured in a flow chart (see Figure 6.1).

Fawcett's ten functional components can be identified in the flow chart: the experiential, logical relationships, negativity and modality relate directly to the knowledge of the universe (modality expresses an 'attitude to the likelihood that a given proposition is true': Fawcett, 1980: 30); the interactional relates to the speaker's intention; the affective to key; the thematic and informational to linguistic context; the metalingual to monitoring; and the discourse organizational partly to the discourse construction program and partly to linguistic context.

2. Intonation in the model

We are now in a position to view the contribution that intonation makes in communication, in a global perspective. In order to help the reader identify that contribution in the communication process, the first person singular will again be used.

A need arises for me to say something.

I have at my disposal a competence in my language which includes all the functions and systems of intonation. I may have a second (or third, etc.) language, in which my competence in intonation may be equal to that in my main, preferred, language; on the other hand, it may be precisely in the area of intonation that I feel one of the limitations in that competence; in fact, my intonation competence may be so seriously defective in that language, that I use wrong patterns altogether and actually distort the message I seek to communicate.

I also have at my disposal a knowledge of the universe which includes an ability to select the most appropriate genre for a particular occasion. On an occasion where informal conversation is appropriate, the prosodic composition of my speech will be adapted to that and I will not sound as if I am reading the news on the radio, or making an announcement at a gathering of several hundred people, or praying, or lecturing, and so on. My use of intonation will help people to identify the **speech style**, or **genre**, that I have selected; see Chapter 1, section 4.6, and Tench (1988, 1990: chapter 7), Crystal and Davy (1969, 1975) and Johns-Lewis (1986).

I decide how much I want to say. If I am participating in an informal conversation, any given turn of mine might consist of a single speech act containing a single piece of information, encoded in a simple intonation unit. On the other hand, I may want to say more than that, two, three, or more intonation units, which will constitute a phonological paragraph. I may wish to extend my turn to two or more phonological paragraphs, in which case the paragraphing structure will become evident. Certainly in an extended monologue, such structure will be evident; it helps people to follow the development of my message, i.e. its textual structure; see Chapter 1, section 4.5 and Tench (1990: chapter 4) and Brazil and Coulthard (1979) and Brazil et al. (1980), Brown and Yule (1983) and Pike (1967).

I decide how I wish to communicate. If I decide to speak, all the functions and systems of intonation are brought into play. Even if I decide to write, intonation still figures in the process. When I am writing a letter, I am often conscious of the way I would speak it: the potential intonation will affect the way I present information, the way I punctuate, the way I might emphasise words or whole propositions and the way I paragraph the material. Even in more formal writing, intonation plays a role; in a scholarly article 'Writing in the perspective of speaking', Chafe (1986) wrote:

> When writing is read aloud, of course, it does have intonation, though the reader may use pitch contours quite different from the spoken norm. The very fact that people assign various kinds of peculiar prosody in reading aloud might suggest that such prosody is invented solely for that purpose, and that written language is, in itself, devoid of intonation, stress, and pauses. But introspection suggests that as both writers and readers we do assign such features to whatever we are writing or reading. For example, when I wrote the last sentence I had in mind a high pitch and strong stress on the word 'do'. You, as reader, may or may not have read it that way, but in either case you are likely to know what you did. I am going to assume that writers and readers assign intonation, stress, and pauses to written language, though the writing itself provides less than optimal representations of them.
>
> Intonation *is*, of course, indicated to *some* extent – often with punctuation, less often with italics. Again I invite you to consider how you read the last sentence. (Chafe, 1986: 18)

This is why the task of identifying the boundaries of intonation units in the opening of *Treasure Island* was not an unreasonable exercise. Robert Louis Stevenson knew that the art of good story-telling in print will match the art of good story-telling in speech. In fact, a high proportion of all written material will reflect the intonational properties of spoken discourse:

> In **speech** each information unit is realized by an **intonation unit**. The equivalent in **writing** is the unit boundaries that are expressed by **punctuation** marks – i.e. commas, dashes, colons and semi-colons within sentences, and full stops ('periods' in US English), question marks and exclamation marks at the ends of sentences.

> From here on we shall focus on intonation rather than punctuation. This is because, even when the text is a written text, the reader tends to read into it the intonation with which it would be spoken if it were read aloud – so that even with a written text it is helpful to understand the meanings built into a spoken text.

> (Fawcett, in preparation; original emphases)

To return to the involvement of intonation in my act of communication, I assess the context of situation. In one very important respect, the setting has to be taken very deliberately into effect. If the addressee is, or addressees are, at some distance from me, I have to call them. The intonation of calling is different from the intonation of settings in which all the participants are within easy, unaided, talking distance. The communication in calling is also different, in that the messages are usually short and the expected responses are equally short. If I call somebody at a distance, especially if I don't know where they are, I raise my voice in both volume and pitch and use two long level pitches, the second usually a semi-tone lower (or two semi-tones lower in repeated calls):

(6.6)   ⁻Jona–than | ⁻Jona_than

Other, familiar, callings include:

(6.7)   ⁻Dinner's –ready

(6.8)   ⁻foo –ood

The pre-tonic is usually kept low, as in:

(6.9)   Come and ⁻get –it

The intonation of calling has not been dealt with in this book until this point; more can be found in Pike (1945: 71–2), Liberman (1979) and Ladd (1980). O'Connor and Arnold (1973) recognize this intonation pattern, pattern 10 ('The terrace') (see p. 115), but they do not illustrate it in any of their drills. This pattern is also known as 'stylized intonation'.

From my assessment of the context of situation, I decide on my communicative intentions, express my feelings and take note of what has been said already. My communicative intentions are expressed through my choice of tone (see Chapter 4, sections 4 and 5), whether I am telling, asking, bidding farewell, and so on. My feelings – if I wish – are expressed through (non-neutral) variations of tones and pre-tonics (see Chapter 5). I note the linguistic (and, at times, the situational) context through choices in tonicity (see Chapter 3), especially in terms of new and given information.

I encode my message as successive pieces of information in intonation units (tonality, see Chapter 2), each unit bearing a focus of information (tonicity, see Chapter 3) and a status in relation to each successive unit (tone, see Chapter 4, section 3). Occasionally, the precise choice in syntactic organization is realized by tonality (see Chapter 2, section 7) and tonicity (see Chapter 3, section 8).

And, finally, when I speak, I give away who I am. I not only give away my views, feelings and intentions, and my perception of the place I occupy in the encounter, but I also give away aspects of my identity: my voice gives away an indication of my gender, age, social class and provenance. There is thus an **indexical** function of intonation (and the rest of my pronunciation) which includes my accent. The indexical function has not been included in the treatment of intonation in this book because it does not directly affect either meaning or paralanguage. It is manifest at the transmission stage of communication. (This is not to deny, however, the possibility that the addressee will evaluate the message in relation to the messenger. This most certainly happens. We might, for instance, doubt the validity of a message when we realize who the messenger is! But that is an operation of the addressee's knowledge of the universe, which is beyond the scope of linguistic description.)

You will see that intonation features at every point in the process of communication; it is impossible to account for any kind of linguistic communication without it. From the process of reception by the addressee to interpretation and evaluation, intonation is recognized, processed and taken into account. Even in writing, and then reading, intonation plays a part.

3. The intonation systems

The foregoing discussion of the contribution of intonation in the whole communication process, and the detailed descriptions of the forms and functions of intonation in English discourse, can all be displayed in a series of system networks. We will make no specific provision for choices in genre and medium, but the choices open to a speaker of English are the following (Figure 6.2a and b):

Discourse construction program

a speaker's turn
- single phonological paragraph
- multiple phonological paragraphs

phonological paragraph
- single intonation unit
- multiple intonation units (intonation group)

Figure 6.2a

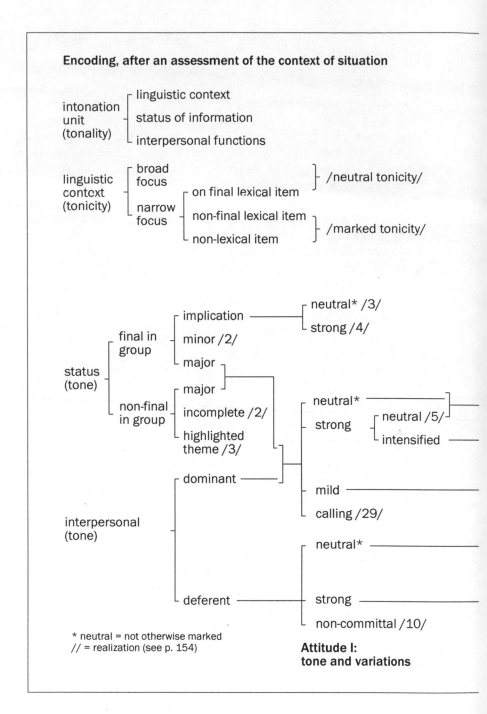

Figure 6.2b

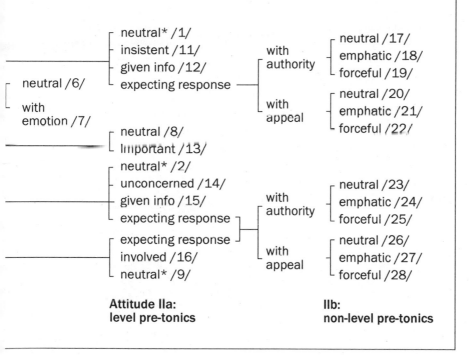

neutral /6/
with
emotion /7/

neutral* /1/
insistent /11/
given info /12/
expecting response

with
authority

neutral /17/
emphatic /18/
forceful /19/

with
appeal

neutral /20/
emphatic /21/
forceful /22/

neutral /8/
important /13/

neutral* /2/
unconcerned /14/
given info /15/
expecting response

with
authority

neutral /23/
emphatic /24/
forceful /25/

expecting response
involved /16/
neutral* /9/

with
appeal

neutral /26/
emphatic /27/
forceful /28/

Attitude IIa:
level pre-tonics

IIb:
non-level pre-tonics

Realizations

	Pre-tonic (if present)	Tone	
1	mid level	neutral fall	They are going to come on ˎMonday
2	mid level	neutral rise	They are going to come on ˊMonday
3	descending	neutral fall-rise	They are going to come on ˅Monday
4	descending glissando	low fall-rise	They are going to come on ˌ˅Monday
5	mid level	high fall	They are going to come on ˋMonday
6	ascending	neutral rise-fall	They are going to come on ʌMonday
7	ascending glissando	low rise-fall	They are going to come on ˌʌMonday
8	mid level	low fall	They are going to come on ˎMonday
9	mid level	high rise	They are going to come on ˊMonday
10	mid level	low rise	They are going to come on ˌMonday
11	high level	neutral/high fall	They are ˉgoing to come on ˎMonday
12	low level	neutral fall	They are ˍgoing to come on ˎMonday
13	high level	low fall	They are ˉgoing to come on ˌMonday
14	low level	neutral/low rise	They are ˍgoing to come on ˊMonday
15	high level	neutral rise	They are ˉgoing to come on ˊMonday
16	low level	high rise	They are ˍgoing to come on ˊMonday
17	descending wide	neutral/high fall	They are ˋgoing to come on ˎMonday
18	descending stepping	neutral/high fall	They are ˉgoing to ˉcome on ˎMonday
19	descending glissando	neutral/high fall	They are ˌgoing to ˌcome on ˎMonday
20	ascending wide	neutral/high fall	They are ˊgoing to come on ˎMonday
21	ascending stepping	neutral/high fall	They are ˍgoing to ˉcome on ˎMonday
22	ascending glissando	neutral/high fall	They are ˊgoing to ˊcome on ˎMonday
23	descending wide	neutral/high rise	They are ˋgoing to come on ˊMonday
24	descending stepping	neutral/high rise	They are ˉgoing to come on ˅Monday
25	descending glissando	neutral/high rise	They are ˌgoing to ˌcome on ˊMonday
26	ascending wide	neutral/high rise	They are ˊgoing to come on ˊMonday
27	ascending stepping	neutral/high rise	They are ˍgoing to ˉcome on ˊMonday
28	ascending glissando	neutral/high rise	They are ˊgoing to ˊcome on ˊMonday
29	low level	high level + mid-high level	They are ˉgoing to come on ˉMon-day

Figure 6.2c

References

Allen, W. Stannard (1954) *Living English Speech*. London: Longmans.

Armstrong, L.C. and Ward, I.C. (1926) *A Handbook of English Intonation* (2nd edn 1931). Cambridge: Heffer.

Baker, A. (1982) *Introducing English Pronunciation: A Teacher's Guide*. Cambridge: CUP.

Bolinger, D.L. (1986) *Intonation and its Parts*. London: Edward Arnold.

Bolinger, D.L. (1988) *Intonation and its Uses*. London: Edward Arnold.

Brazil, D. (1975) *Discourse Intonation I*. University of Birmingham: English Language Research.

Brazil, D. (1978) *Discourse Intonation II*. University of Birmingham: English Language Research.

Brazil, D, and Coulthard, M. (1979) *Exchange Structure*, University of Birmingham: English Language Research.

Brazil, D., Coulthard, M. and Johns, C. (1980) *Discourse Intonation and Language Teaching*. London: Longman.

Brown, G. (1977) *Listening to Spoken English* (2nd edn 1990). London: Longman.

Brown, G., Currie, K. and Kenworthy, J. (1980) *Questions of Intonation*. London: Croom Helm.

Brown, G. and Yule, G. (1983) *Discourse Analysis*. Cambridge: CUP.

Brown, P. and Fraser, C. (1979) 'Speech as a marker of situation' in Scherer, K.R. and Giles, H. (eds), *Social Markers in Speech*. Cambridge: CUP.

Chafe, W. (1986) 'Writing in the perspective of speaking' in Cooper, R. and Greenbaum, S. (eds), *Studying Writing*. London: Sage.

Couper-Kuhlen, E. (1986) *An Introduction to English Prosody*. London: Edward Arnold.

Cruttenden, A. (1986) *Intonation*. Cambridge: CUP.

Crystal, D. (1969) *Prosodic Systems and Intonation in English*. Cambridge: CUP.

Crystal, D. (1975) *The English Tone of Voice*. London: Edward Arnold.

Crystal, D. and Davy, D. (1969) *Investigating English Style*. London: Longman.

Crystal, D. and Davy, D. (1975) *Advanced Conversational English*. London: Longman.

Dickinson, L. and Mackin, R. (1969) *Varieties of Spoken English*. Oxford: OUP.

Fawcett, R.P. (1980) *Cognitive Linguistics and Social Interaction*. Heidelberg: Julius Groos; Exeter: Exeter University.

Fawcett, R.P. (in preparation) *Handbook for the Analysis of Sentences in English Text*, Vol. 1: *Syntax. A Systemic Functional Approach*. Extracts available from Computational Linguistics Unit, University of Wales, Cardiff CF1 3TL.

Gibbon, D. (1976) *Perspectives on Intonation Analysis*. Frankfurt am Main: Peter Lang.

Giles, H. and Coupland, N. (1991) *Language: Contexts and Consequences*. Milton Keynes: Open UP.

Giles, H. and Hewstone, M. (1982) 'Cognitive structures, speech and social situations: two integrative models', *Language Sciences* 4: 187–219.

References

Gimson, A.C. (1989) *An Introduction to the Pronunciation of English*, 4th edn. London: Edward Arnold.

Halliday, M.A.K. (1967) *Intonation and Grammar in British English*. The Hague: Mouton.

Halliday, M.A.K. (1970) *A Course in Spoken English: Intonation*. London: Oxford UP.

Halliday, M.A.K. (1973) *Explorations in the Functions of Language*. London: Edward Arnold.

Halliday, M.A.K. (1978) *Language as Social Semiotic*. London: Edward Arnold.

Halliday, M.A.K. (1985) *An Introduction to Functional Grammar*. London: Edward Arnold.

Halliday, M.A.K. and Hasan, R. (1985) *Language, Context, and Text*. Oxford: OUP.

Halliday, M.A.K., McIntosh, A. and Strevens, P. (1964) *The Linguistic Sciences and Language Teaching*. London: Longman.

Hooke, R. and Rowell, J. (1982) *A Handbook of English Pronunciation*. London: Edward Arnold.

Hudson, R.A. (1975) 'The meaning of questions', *Language* 51: 1–31.

Hymes, D. (1977) *Foundations in Sociolinguistics*. London: Tavistock.

Johns-Lewis, C. (1986) 'Prosodic differentiation of discourse modes' in Johns-Lewis, C. (ed.), *Intonation in Discourse*. London: Croom Helm.

Joos, M. (1961) *The Five Clocks*. New York: Harcourt, Brace and World.

Kingdon, R. (1958) *The Groundwork of English Intonation*. London: Longman.

Knowles, G. (1989) *Patterns of Spoken English*. London: Longman.

Ladd, D.R. (1980) *The Structure of Intonational Meaning*. Bloomington: Indiana UP.

Ladd, D.R. (1983) 'Phonological features of intonational peaks', *Language* 59: 721–59.

Lee, W.R. (1956) 'English intonation: a new approach', *Lingua* 5: 345–71.

Leech, G. and Svartvik, J. (1994) *A Communicative Grammar of English*, 2nd edn. London: Longman.

Lehiste, I. (1975) 'The phonetic structure of paragraphs in Cohen, A. and Nooteboom, S. G. (eds), *Structure and Process in Speech Perception*. Berlin: Springer.

Lehiste, I. (1979) 'Perception of sentence and paragraph boundaries' in Lindblom, B. and Ohman, S. (eds), *Frontiers of Speech Research*. London: Academic Press.

Liberman, M. (1979) *The Intonational System of English*. New York/London: Garland.

O'Connor, J.D. and Arnold, G.F. (1961) *Intonation of Colloquial English* (2nd edn 1973). London: Longman.

Palmer, H.E. (1922) *English Intonation (with Systematic Exercises)*. Cambridge: Heffer.

Pike, K.L. (1945) *The Intonation of American English*. Ann Arbor: University of Michigan Press.

Pike, K.L. (1967) *Language in Relation to a Unified Theory of the Structure of Human Behavior*, 2nd edn. The Hague: Mouton.

Quirk, R., Duckworth, A.P., Svartvik, J., Rusiecki, J.P.L. and Colin, A.J.T. (1964) 'Studies in the correspondence of prosodic to grammatical features of English', *Proc. Ling.* IX: 679–91.

Quirk, R., Greenbaum, S., Leech, G. and Svartvik, J. (1972) *A Grammar of Contemporary English*. London: Longman.

Roach, P. (1983) *English Phonetics and Phonology* (2nd edn 1991). Cambridge: CUP.

Schubiger, M. (1958) *English Intonation, its Form and Function*. Tübingen: Niemeyer.

Sinclair, J. McH. (1972) *A Course in Spoken English: Grammar*. London: Oxford UP.

Taglicht, J. (1984) *Message and Emphasis: On Focus and Scope in English*. London: Longman.

Tench, P. (1988) 'The stylistic potential of intonation' in Coupland, N. (ed.), *Styles of Discourse*. London: Croom Helm.

Tench, P. (1990) *The Roles of Intonation in English Discourse*. Frankfurt am Main: Peter Lang.

Thompson, I. (1981) *Intonation Practice*. Oxford: OUP.

Wells, W.H.G. (1986) 'An experimental approach to the interpretation of focus in spoken English' in Johns-Lewis, C. (ed.), *Intonation in Discourse*. London: Croom Helm.

Young, D. (1980) *The Structure of English Clauses*. London: Hutchinson.

Index

___